Teaching Mathematics through Reading

Methods and Materials for Grades 6-8

Faith H. Wallace, PhD
and Jill Shivertaker

Linworth
Books

Professional Development Resources for K-12
Library Media and Technology Specialists

Library of Congress Cataloging-in-Publication Data

Wallace, Faith H.
  Teaching mathematics through reading : methods and materials for grades 6-8 / Faith H. Wallace and Jill Shivertaker.
     p. cm.
  Includes bibliographical references and index.
  ISBN-13: 978-1-58683-324-4 (pbk.)
  ISBN-10: 1-58683-324-3 (pbk.)
  1. Mathematics--Study and teaching (Middle school) 2. Reading--Study and teaching (Middle school) 3. Literacy--Study and teaching (Middle school) I. Shivertaker, Jill. II. Title.
  QA11.2.W35 2008
  510.71'2--dc22

                          2008022039

Cynthia Anderson: Editor
Carol Simpson: Editorial Director
Judi Repman: Consulting Editor

Published by Linworth Publishing, Inc.
3650 Olentangy River Road
Suite 250
Columbus, Ohio 43214

ISBN 13: 978-158683-324-4
ISBN 10: 1-58683-324-3

5 4 3 2 1

Table of Contents

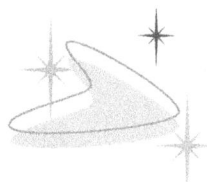

Figures and Tables

Figures

Tables

About the Authors

Faith H. Wallace, PhD *(faithwallace@earthlink.net)* is an assistant professor of adolescent education and literacy at Kennesaw State University in Kennesaw, Georgia. Dr. Wallace has been an active member of the University System of Georgia's Reading Consortium for over five years. Her research interests include content area literacy, adolescent literature, and professional development of literacy teachers. Her work has been published in *Mathematics Teaching in the Middle School* and *The Journal of Content Area Reading*. Visit her Web site: <http://ksuweb.kennesaw.edu/~fwallac1/>.

Jill Shivertaker is a sixth-grade mathematics teacher at Lovinggood Middle School in Cobb County, Georgia. Jill received a BS from the University of Florida and a BS in Middle Grades Education from Kennesaw State University. An avid reader, and a senior programmer/analyst prior to her transition to the classroom, her focus is to incorporate both reading and technology into the curriculum. At home she enjoys spending time with her husband and two children, tap dancing, and DDR.

Acknowledgments

We wish to thank, first, our husbands who were often subjected to trying our activities. Without Faith's husband Ken, the baseball activity might never have made it into the book. In addition, thank you to Mary Hadjuk for her reviews. Finally, we thank Dr. Marj Economopolous, Dr. Lynn Stallings, and Dr. Karen Koellner for their constant feedback and support.

Chapter 1

Introduction

More than 10 years ago, I, Faith Wallace, was teaching English language arts at a neighborhood school in suburban New Jersey. I cherished those classes where we read and wrote amazing novels, stories, plays, poetry—anything I could find, even song lyrics. Of course, that makes sense; it was an English class. We discussed everything: summarizing, synthesizing, analyzing. Then one day, I started thinking about *transfer*. Would my students be able to transfer our classroom experiences to other classes and to life in general? Would they take what they had learned and apply it in new situations? One Wednesday I had an idea; it would be *Wacky Word Problem Day*. Instead of our normal discussions, I posed math story problems based on our reading. The students panicked. Complaints erupted. "This isn't math class," they demanded. That's when my passion for mathematical literacy began and continues to grow and flourish (Wallace and Clark; Wallace, Clark, and Cherry). When I met Jill Shivertaker she was taking one of my college courses that encourages the use of print in all classrooms. Jill was so empowered by the idea that she, a math teacher, began creating unique and sophisticated activities for the middle grades mathematics classroom. We worked together as we shared readings and suggestions, thoughts and questions. The result is this book.

Reading and mathematics naturally balance themselves in life (Steen). When was the last time—really think about it—you didn't need to apply number sense and reading in your everyday life? It could be a currency issue, instructions for an appliance or an advanced toy, a recipe, a transit schedule, interest rates, late fees, a lottery ticket, distance, membership configurations, taxes…middle grades students need to start seeing the natural connection between math and their lives now and later as consumers in a democratic society. We believe when you start including diverse text in the math classroom, you do just that. Both the National Council of Teachers of English (NCTE) and the National Council of Teachers of Mathematics (NCTM) agree that reading across the curriculum only enriches instruction in all content areas.

Why middle grades? Simple. Middle grades students are often overlooked when it comes to the integration of mathematics and reading. The majority of the resources for librarians and teachers target young audiences, typically K-4, but sometimes as far as 6th grade (Whitin and Wilde; Martinez and Martinez). Even if librarians and teachers used these books as guides they would not usually include upper grades topics such as variables, equations, statistics and graphing, probability, and measures of central tendency.

Thus, there are two sections to this book. The first section, Chapters 1 through 4, introduces three types of text: informational trade books, literature, and environmental print. For each text type, we also provide annotated bibliographies and lists of potential resources. In these chapters we hope library media specialists and teachers alike will find a wealth of materials to include in school and classroom libraries. We offer suggestions when to purchase class sets and when to have a few books in the media center. We hope that math teachers will bring their students to the library to see that there are math books available to them for reading in the math classroom and for their own research and enjoyment.

In section two, Chapters 5 through 9, we provide activities using these types of texts. The activities use the different types of texts in a number of different ways. Where possible, we suggest using the library in several lessons. But, this section is primarily for teachers to get them started using reading in the mathematics classroom.

In addition, a unique feature of this book is that we offer *detailed* lesson plans for teachers, complete with reproducibles that might be needed. This book was planned not to make teaching mathematics harder, but to make teaching mathematics richer. As a bonus, we include an appendix of current mathematical picture books that we believe could hold a place in the school and classroom library. Finally, we include a full bibliography at the end of the text.

A careful eye will notice that we said we cover all of the Content Standards of NCTM. The reason that we did not include the Process Standards is that we have problem solving, reasoning and proof, communication, representation, and connections in each activity. But, to be fair, we offer this lighthearted problem-solving activity here in the introduction.

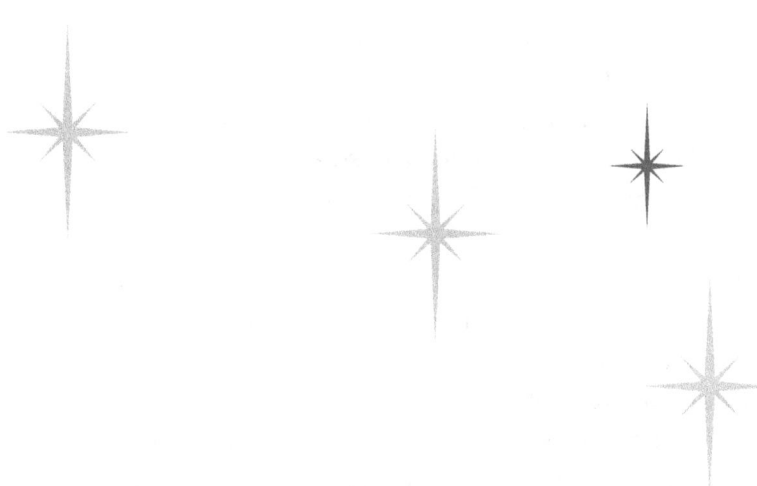

Activity 1: Who Ate the Cheese?   ? ? ?

Objective: Students will work to solve a logic problem with only partial information coming from a section of reading. However, with the right strategy, they can solve the problem.

Materials & Preparation:

1. Easel/Poster paper and markers
2. Collins, Suzanne. *Gregor and the Code of Claw*. New York: Scholastic, 2007, pp.132-134.

Estimated Time: 30-60 minutes

NCTM Standard:

Process Standards: Solve problems that arise in mathematics and in other contexts; apply and adapt a variety of appropriate strategies to solve problems; communicate their mathematical thinking coherently and clearly to peers.

Activity Instructions:

1. Organize students into groups of 3-4.

2. Provide a copy of the text to each group/student. Read the section aloud and ask students to circle unknown words. Help students define unknown words.

3. Have the groups read the section again. *Ask students to identify possible clues or helpful information as they read by underlining or highlighting;* then organize their data. The groups should come up with the following or similar chart (Table 1.1).

Method used:	Clues:	Who ate cheese?	Problems:
guess	7 creatures	roach	What's a mammal?
drew a diagram	7 foods	bat	Which are mammals?
created a table	no one had the same food	rat	not enough info
Venn diagram	the bat's favorite foods	mouse	can't eliminate
made a list	what the roach didn't like	rat	none
	mouse did not eat cheese	rat	
	Underlander's favorites		
	what the mammals didn't eat		
	Overlander's favorites		

Table 1.1: Data from Gregor and the Code of the Claw

Activity 1: Who Ate the Cheese? continued

1. Compare the groups' methods and answers. Use inquiry to question the class and elicit a dialogue about problem solving.

   a. "Which group had the best method for solving the problem? Why?"

   b. "Is there a *best* method for solving problems?"

   c. "What other information do we need?"

   d. "If you guessed, what would be the probability that you would get the answer correct?"

   e. "How is solving a problem like this one related to math?"

The correct answers are shown in the completed solve chart in Table 1.2.

Answer to the Riddle

	Overlander	Underlander	bat	mouse	roach non-mammal	spider non-mammal	rat
fish	x	x	x	•	x	x	x
cheese	x	x	x	x	x	x	•
cake	x	x	•	x	x	x	x
cookies	x	x	x	x	x	•	x
bread	•	x	x	x	x	x	x
mushrooms	x	x	x	x	•	x	x
shrimp	x	•	x	x	x	x	x

Table 1.2: Answer to the Riddle

Chapter 2

Informational Trade Books

With the Internet at our fingertips, never before has information been so readily available to students, teachers, parents...most anyone, and on nearly any topic imaginable. In fact, Faith was watching the hit television medical drama *House M.D.*, and heard a haunting song in the background. Through careful searching, she found that very song on the Internet and was able to listen to it. During that search, she also found a very interesting book entitled, *The Facts Behind the Addictive Medical Drama: The Medical Science of House, M.D.* (Holtz) that she purchased and read: an *informational trade book*.

The Internet is not the only method for gleaning information about particularly interesting topics (or *any* topic for that matter); books continue to be published on topics far and wide. These are often labeled informational trade books. Informational trade books are nonfiction (factual) and feature detailed, compelling, and often little known information about a given topic. Such books are written for a general public audience: children, young adults, adults; not specifically for school and academics. The books don't follow curriculum guides or testing materials. That means the author is passionate about the content and wants to convey that passion to other interested readers. In this way, trade books present otherwise technical or academic information in ways that grab and keep the reader's attention. Informational trade books can provide captivating illustrations and link pertinent information to everyday life.

Informational trade books are not limited to a particular format. Trade books can be chapter books (by single or multiple authors), picture books, activity books, or photographic books. It is important to remember that these are formats, not levels. For example, a picture book could be extremely complex; it just happens to have a copious amount of pictures to supplement the text.

Informational trade books can be incredibly useful in math classrooms. Trade books have been written on the history of the number zero, on speculations of the importance of pi, and about famous mathematicians. Trade books are flexible; you can use an excerpt, a chapter from a book, the entire book—whatever works for your lesson. Here, we present a number of trade books that have useful and intriguing mathematical information. Remember to preview all readings before using them in class to determine appropriateness.

Dollar Bill Origami (Montroll)

In this activity book, students learn how to make a variety of origami figures, including three-dimensional figures, using just a one-dollar bill. Math teachers will appreciate the information provided on page 10 about creating a square. All directions provide visuals and would be a great addition to a geometry classroom. Multiple copies of this book would be necessary so students could work in groups to make projects. This is something that can be done in the media center or individual classroom.

Go Figure! A Totally Cool Book about Numbers (Ball)

This picture book is packed with activities that let you experience the magic of numbers. Brainteasers, magic tricks, and mind-reading games are included. Mathematics topics such as the history of counting, Fibonacci, golden ratio, infinity, primes, pi, and more are discussed. Multiple copies of this book in the library would be prudent. A class set of *Go Figure!* would be ideal since it can be used for so many different projects.

If You Hopped Like a Frog (Schwartz)

This deceptively sophisticated picture book focuses on ratio and proportion and compares creatures in our world with humans. The last four pages give students an opportunity to figure out ratio and proportion with other animals and objects. If you enjoy this book, try *If Dogs Were Dinosaurs* by the same author. This author has several books of similar type. Plan to purchase multiple copies of each. Once a teacher uses these books in the classroom, students are going to want to check them out of the library.

The Joy of Pi (Blatner)

What is pi? Why is it so elusive? Will there ever be a final number for pi? Find out the answers to all of these questions and more in *The Joy of Pi*. Blatner traces the history of the interest in pi and how progress was made to understand this important concept. The book is peppered with jokes, anecdotes, and activities to keep the reader's attention. This is a more sophisticated, but interesting, book. One copy in the classroom library and media center would be enough.

Math Stuff (Pappas)

This chapter book is invaluable to the middle grades classroom. In short chapters, Pappas showcases ways in which mathematics is part of everyday life. She touches on art, nature, and computers, to name a few topics. One particularly interesting section displays "number systems and symbols used over the centuries" (p. 86). She even talks about math and virtual reality. A great deal of teaching topics can come from this book. We recommend a classroom set of Pappas' book.

Mathematicians Are People, Too: Stories from the Lives of Great Mathematicians (Reimer and Reimer)

This book of biographies includes Archimedes, Napier, Newton, Germain, and more. The biographies are written in a story-like fashion with relevant mathematics included within the stories. Topics within the biographies include geometry, algebra, measurement, and women in mathematics. Purchase at least one copy for the biography section.

Moneyball: The Art of Winning an Unfair Game (Lewis)

How do you win in the Major Leagues with a tight budget? This book describes in detail how new ways of interpreting statistical data are better for evaluating players and predicting wins than the old philosophies such as simply looking at a hitter's batting average and home runs or a pitcher's wins, losses or saves. Anyone who loves baseball will love this information text because it reads like a narrative and delves deep into the heart of the sport. Multiple copies for the classroom and media center would be prudent.

Numbers (Boyle and Roddick)

In sections that talk about mathematical maps of the stars, ratio and proportion of salaries around the world, and the biggest numbers in the world, the authors present interesting (and sometimes startling) numbers. For example, "If Barbie were human, she'd be 7 feet 2 inches tall, with a neck twice as long as normal and the measurements 39-23-33" (p. 53). We suggest just a classroom copy of this facts and figures book.

Squares: Shapes in Math, Science, and Nature (Ross)

Everything you need to teach squares to young adults is in this simple and easy-to-read format. Topics include properties, history, construction, and use of squares in puzzles, city planning, and art. Detailed activities utilize tangrams, origami, pentominoes, cubes, and painting. The color and illustrations make this book an enjoyable read, and there are many ways to use it for interdisciplinary projects. It's a must-have for a classroom set.

Women and Numbers: Lives of Women Mathematicians plus Discovery Activities (Perl)

This is a compilation of 13 biographies of women mathematicians from 1780 to the present, including Lovelace, Blum, and Pappas. Within each biography the author includes the mathematician's approaches to problems, as well as her ambitions and techniques. In addition, there are activities and illustrations throughout the book. At least one copy of Perl's book should be in the biography section of the media center.

Why Do Buses Come in Threes? The Hidden Mathematics of Everyday Life (Eastaway and Wyndham)

Eastaway and Wyndham bring mathematics to our everyday life. They organize this chapter book by questions: "What's the best way to cut a cake?" "How many people watch *Friends*?" The questions are posed to discuss the math we don't see. Each chapter answers the question and provides interesting sidebars and little-known details such as how many men wear skirts. This is a more complex text, but a fascinating one at that. Once students start reading about the quirky uses for mathematics, they may be inclined to want to read more. We suggest a classroom and media center copy.

Chapter 3

Literature

When we deliver presentations about linking literature and mathematics, teachers are skeptical. They perceive reading as a subject that is outside the realm of teaching mathematics, something extra (even superfluous) that would take away too much time from teaching math. That's a shame. Literature can be a way to engage students in learning mathematics. That is, mathematics is part of our everyday lives. Thus, literature telling authentic stories is bound to grapple with mathematical conundrums. In this way, students have a chance to *enjoy* learning mathematics. Literature does this for students. Further, literature provides students with opposing viewpoints, cultural diversity, and abstract concepts. Either way, students will be sure to have a rich dialogue in the mathematics classroom regarding any assigned reading.

Above all, literature should be read for enjoyment; that should be the primary goal in selecting a piece of literature for the mathematics classrooms. For the purpose of this book, we define literature as narrative text that tells a fictional or semi-fictional story. Once students are engaged in the text, lessons and discussions regarding mathematics will naturally take place. Moreover, there are many ways to use literature in the mathematics classroom: as a teacher read-aloud, as a whole class reading, in the form of using specific excerpts, and as independent reading on a classroom library shelf. For example, *The Midnighters* series by Scott Westerfield is an action-packed fantasy where multiples of 13 are critical. In these books, the number 13 is quite special, and anything that is linked to the number serves as protection for a group of young adults. The series is fast-paced and action-packed from start to finish, so a few excerpts read aloud in class may actually encourage students to read the series on their own. Who knows? Students may even come to you with questions about multiples.

Since we emphasize that literature should be read for enjoyment, the books on our list are good works of fiction. There is no reason to keep these books only for the math classroom. Everyone could find a book on this list that they might like to read. Having each in the library would be beneficial to all students.

If teachers are familiar with mathematical literature for young adults, it is the staples: *The Phantom Tollbooth* (Juster), *The Toothpaste Millionaire* (Merrill), and *The Number Devil: A Mathematical Adventure* (Enzensberger). The following titles are, we hope, the next generation of staples for mathematical literature. As always, it is of *extreme importance* that teachers read these books prior to using them in their classrooms to determine their appropriateness and educational value.

A Gebra Named Al (Isdell)

This charming fantasy adventure has a student transported to the Land of Mathematics. Her journey to see the great Mathematician in Higher Mathematics is filled with mathematical and scientific knowledge. Most of the problems deal with order of operations; in fact, there is a cave that the characters walk through in such a way as to represent working with parenthesis. This book reads more like an entertaining textbook, and can be used as a whole-class reading due to the content and the length. Therefore, a class set of books would be ideal.

All of the Above (Pearsall)

Based on a true story, this book written by the Newbery Honor-author tells the story of four adolescents' struggle to construct the world's largest tetrahedron as part of a math project at urban Washington Middle School. The characters each face their own personal challenges at home and in life. Written by the teacher and students themselves, the book provides a protagonist that a varied audience can relate to, and positive insight into the world in which they live. The math project gives readers a peek into Serpinski's Tetrahedron with a brief discussion of its properties. This book is a fast read, and can be a read-aloud while working on a geometry unit. A class set would be great, especially if it is housed in the library where other students can pick it up.

An Abundance of Katherines (Green)

When yet another girl named Katherine dumps Colin Singleton, he decides to look at relationships in a different way: mathematically. Colin and his best friend Hassan hit the road and discover the effects variables can have on life and mathematical formulas. While most of the math in this buddy adventure is humorous and quirky, an appendix written by a university professor applies mathematical reasoning to Colin's ideas. Thus, the book can be an entertaining read and an informational journey. Green's book is just plain fun, and should be read that way. Have a copy in the classroom library and media center and do a good booktalk!

Artifacts (Evans)

Artifacts was recognized as an adult novel with young adult appeal. This mystery features archaeologist Faye Longchamp, whose profession requires her to use mathematics and science concepts to help her reconstruct the past. Faye and her friend Joe use geometry to pinpoint a killer's motive, to document a crime scene, and to track down buried treasure; knowledge of parabolic flight paths helps them find a key piece of evidence. *School Library Journal* said that Mary Anna Evans' work will "engage the imagination of readers." Of all the books on our list, these most successfully cross all curriculum including science and social studies. Mary Anna has two other books, *Relics* and *Effigies,* which also include mathematical content. Since *Artifacts* is a truly cross-curricular book, we suggest a class set, and we encourage you to put together an integrated unit with all subjects in which students read the book in English class, and then explore the math, science, and social studies aspects in the other classrooms.

Big Slick: High Stakes and Dirty Laundry (Luper)

After 16-year-old Andrew takes a bad beat in an underground local Texas Hold 'Em tournament, he loses money that wasn't his. And he needs to figure out a way to pay it back as quickly as possible. Along the way, Andrew, with help from his best-friend Scott and Goth-chick co-worker Jasmine, makes some bad choices and some really bad choices. While most of the math deals with calculating pot odds or the likelihood that Andrew will flop a much-needed King, it fits seamlessly within the story and helps you play along with Andrew as he wins some and loses some in this fast-paced adventure. Another fun book to have in the classroom library and media center since poker is so popular these days.

Chasing Vermeer (Balliett)

Two teens work to discover where a famous painting has been hidden. Suspicious activity in their neighborhood, even by their teacher, leads them to believe the painting is close by. Mathematics is a natural part of the plot line. In fact, one of the characters uses pentominoes, a mathematical manipulative, to help him solve his problems. The sequel, *The Wright 3*, incorporates a great deal more mathematics including geometry and the Fibonacci sequence. These are extremely engaging books that students will enjoy as independent reading. Both are great books to have in the classroom library and media center. The sequel may warrant a class set.

"Different Kinds of Darkness" (Langford)

What if mathematics could be deadly? Find out in this short story (from the book of the same title) in which mathematics can short-circuit your brain. This is a perfect read-aloud in a mathematics class studying fractals.

Evil Genius (Jinks)

Where do villains go to learn their trade? In *Evil Genius* we get a glimpse into the education of evil geniuses at Axis Institute. Mathematics abounds, from ciphers and algorithms to equations and encryptions. At the heart of *Evil Genius* is the story of Cadel Darkkon, the son of the ultimate evil genius who continues to manipulate Cadel's life while in jail. Cadel's life is turned upside-down once he enters Axis Institute, where he learns that nothing is what it seems. A great booktalk, and everyone will want to read this book. It is excellent. Buy plenty!

The Green Glass Sea (Klages)

Fact and fiction are blended in this coming-of-age novel written from the naïve perspective of two young girls whose parents work on the creation of the atom bomb. Both girls, considered outcasts, struggle to fit in with the other children living in this secret society in New Mexico in 1943. There are limited references to actual mathematical problems but famous mathematicians and physicists (such as Enrico Fermi and J. Robert Oppenheimer) are brought to life, which make for interesting cross-curriculum reading. Purchase at least one copy for the classroom library and media center. It's a good booktalk choice that will spark some interest for those who like historical fiction.

A Higher Geometry (Moranville)

At a time when girls were expected to get married and have children, Anna longs to go to school to study mathematics. Can she become the mathematician she longs to be? In this piece of historical fiction, the story provides a glimpse into the life of a young woman in the male-dominated world of the 1950s. Math is sprinkled throughout the book. Math contests and qualifying exams near the end of the book provide trigonometry problems and geometry proofs and theorems. Purchase at least one copy for the classroom library and media center. It's a good booktalk choice that will spark some interest will for those who like historical fiction.

Jayden's Rescue (Tumanov)

Three teens find a magical book where a princess has been captured. As they try to save the princess, they encounter numerous obstacles—all in the form of mathematical riddles. Much like *A Gebra Named Al*, this book feels like an engaging textbook. The length and number of mathematical challenges makes it manageable for a whole-class reading.

Lunch Money (Clements)

Two teens compete in schemes for earning money at school. The ultimate competition surfaces when both start writing and selling comic books. What begins as a bitter competition becomes a team effort between the teens with the help of their mathematics teacher. In an interesting twist, the mathematics teacher thinks through everything as a math problem. Purchase at least one copy for the classroom library and media center. It's a good booktalk choice that will spark some interest for those budding entrepreneurs.

Midnighters: The Secret Hour (Westerfield)

The number 13 usually conjures up feelings of dread. Not in this fantasy adventure. Thirteen is a sign of protection. Multiples of 13 and even longitude and latitude equaling 13 are critical for safety. *The Secret Hour* is the first book in a trilogy. In the second book, math enthusiast Dess provides content which is interwoven throughout the story: using a GPS device useful for "turning Bixby into numbers..."; describing the coordinates as x and y; a reference to the two- and three-dimensional world in Abbott's groundbreaking math-based novel *Flatland*; the ability to work in base two and base sixty; and the underlying presence of the number thirteen, either the number itself or as a factor or multiple, as a common element integral to the plot. The last book in the series continues to focus on numbers and mathematics, but also incorporates physics. These are popular books so have several copies on hand. Give a good booktalk about the blue hour, and your fantasy fans will dive in. Be sure you have the complete trilogy, though.

Mind Games (Grunwell)

A group of students in an afternoon club concoct a science experiment to determine if extrasensory perception is possible. The book traces their entire data analysis process. A good lesson on the law of averages is embedded within the story. We recommend buying a class set and pairing this reading with the science class because of the crossover of science and math within the storyline.

Millions (Boyce)

Two brothers find a fortune of money that was on a train bound for destruction. The brothers take and hide the money and try to use their newfound "millions" without getting caught, but in the process, they learn about the concept of inflation. While economics usually has its place in the social studies classroom, the concept of "value" is an integral component of mathematics. Also, the currency used in the book is British Pounds, which lends itself to a lesson on currency conversion. Purchase at least one copy for the classroom library and media center. It's a good booktalk choice that will spark some interest for those who love money. A movie version was released by Fox Spotlight Pictures in 2005 directed by Danny Boyle, and is now available on DVD.

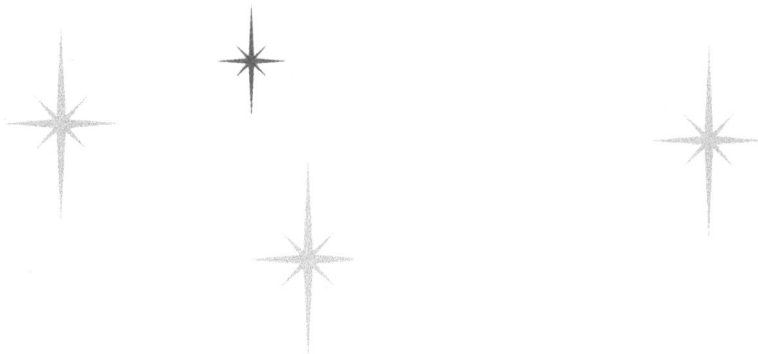

Chapter 4

Environmental Print

We live in a print-rich environment, from mailboxes full of catalogs, solicitations, and advertisements to a hand-written note stuffed under the windshield wiper of your car. Now, we also have spam bypassing filters to enter our e-mail accounts. Information exchanges daily in myriad modes. All of this print is considered *environmental print*. Environmental print is real-time text that occurs naturally within our environment such as advertisements and lottery tickets. Environmental print often contains rich mathematics, links to everyday life, as well as sociopolitical and consumer issues. Additionally, reading and making meaning takes on an important role because students read environmental print for a variety of purposes, and fine print may be involved. Environmental print allows students to connect the power that mathematical understanding can have on their everyday lives.

Young adults are often the targets of consumer-related environmental print such as coupons, advertisements, and payment plans. All of these pieces of text have fine print that needs to be read carefully or the consumer may be misinformed, let down, or worse, swindled. Environmental print infused in mathematics lessons supports students becoming informed citizens in a consumer society. Take lottery tickets, for instance: few people, if any, carefully read the fine print on the back of the ticket. Coupons for stores often have stipulations in which you have to make a choice on the discount to be applied. For many of us, we don't learn this until we are at the counter ready to make our purchases.

The highlight of using environmental print for learning is that it is so naturally and regularly available. Here is a list of possible choices:

- Lottery Tickets
- Coupons
- Advertisements
- Street Signs
- Directions
- Credit Card Solicitations

- Nutritional Information (e.g. cereal box)
- Receipts
- Billboards
- Spam
- Terms and Conditions

- Flyers
- Anything that says *Free Offer*
- Menus
- Catalogs

Methods & Materials

In this section we build on the first three chapters and present activities using some of the already suggested text types and others that are suitable. Each activity is arranged and supported by the National Council of Mathematics Teacher's standards represented in Table 4.1.

Content Standards	Mathematical concepts should not be dealt with in isolation, the concepts should overlap. We focus on the following content standards
Number and Operation	Scientific Notation x 10 Create an equitable ranking system Develop algorithms Compare offers to determine the best offer
Algebra	Cipher systems: crypt and encryption codes Tetrahedrons Represent and analyze functions in society
Geometry	Create a variety of shapes with everyday products Determine trajectory Prefixes and word parts Rotational and line symmetry
Measurement	Determine scale factors Conversion of currency; write formulas to more easily convert Area and perimeter of sports arenas
Data Analysis and Probability	Compare student perception of data with actual data Use data and various math applications to solve a mystery A mathematical science experiment
Process Standards	Problem solving should be intertwined with the above topics
Problem Solving	Logic Problem

The NCTM standards are described in more detail at <www.nctm.org/standards/>.

Table 4.1 NCTM Content Standards

Chapter 5

Numbers and Operations

Activity 5.1: Scientific Notation x 10?
(Informational Trade Book)

Objective: Students will read excerpts from an informational text to find relevant applications of large numbers and express those numbers in scientific notation. Students will also practice entering the values in a calculator and find other real-world data containing large numbers.

Materials & Preparation:

1. Worksheet

2. Roberts, David, ed. *Pick Me Up: Stuff You Need to Know....* New York: DK Publishing, 2006.

3. Calculators (optional)

Estimated Time: 30-45 minute homework activity/review

Activity 5.1: Scientific Notation x 10? continued

Activity Instructions:

1. *Pick Me Up* is the modern-day encyclopedia. It is a rich text, covering a wide variety of topics and in a format suitable for students raised in the era of the Internet, instant messaging, and scrolling news bites. Each page provides a snippet of information: a top 10 list, pictogram, recipe, illustration, diagram, or table. It is most comprehensive and has a place in every classroom and subject.

2. For the purposes of an activity on scientific notation, several excerpts have been pieced together to provide significant numbers as a source for homework questions.

3. Also, an introduction and review of scientific notation should be conducted with a larger discussion on why scientific notation is helpful for expressing very large (and very small) numbers.

4. The worksheet also lends itself to some practice in converting between units (feet-inches-yards) and comparisons of metric and English customary units.

5. As a final question the teacher could provide for a small research activity in the media center using the Internet, TV news, or a book to find a factoid with a large number in it (such as population statistics, distance, number of cells in human body, gross ticket sales of a popular movie). Remind students that a "factoid" means it is factual information. As a warm-up activity, the found information can be shared with the class.

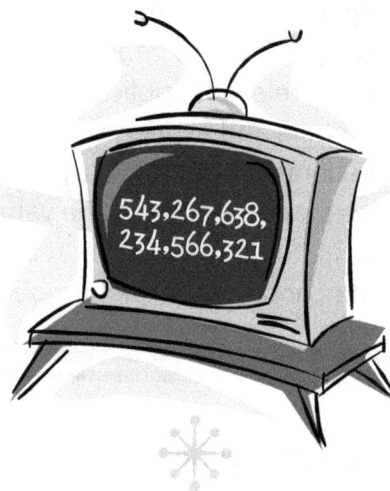

543,267,638, 234,566,321

Scientific Notation x 10²

PRIME NUMBERS

"761 is a prime number. By reversing it, you get the prime number 167. This sort of number is called an emirp (prime spelled backward)."

"1,000,000,000 is called a billion in the United States, but is still sometimes known as a milliard in Europe."

"5! means factorial 5, or 1x2x3x4x5 = 120. The factorial of 10 (10!) is 3,628,800."

– Pick Me Up, p. 212

Write the numbers in scientific notation:

1. 761 = _____

2. 167 = _____

3. 1,000,000,000 = _____

4. 3,628,800 = _____

EARTH

"Diameter: 7,926 miles (12,800 km). Average distance from sun: 93,000,000 miles."

"If you want to be at the top of the world, go to Mt. Everest and climb the 29,035 ft (8,850 m) to the summit."

"If you could find scales big enough, it's reckoned that Earth would weigh in at nearly 6,000,000,000,000,000,000,000,000 metric tons. Heavy, man."

– Pick Me Up, pp. 168-171

Write the numbers in scientific notation:

5. 7,926 = _____

6. 12,800 = _____

7. 93,000,000 = _____

8. 29,035 = _____

9. 8,850 = _____

10. 6,000,000,000,000,000,000,000,000 = _____

GOOGOL

A googol is 1×10^{100}

11. Express 1.9×10^7 as a number: _____. This is the number of humans in Australia!

12. Express 9.9×10^7 as a number: _____. This is the number of sheep in Australia!

13. Express 6.5956×10^6 as a number in the blank: Russia is the largest country in the world...its total area is _____ sq. miles.

– *Pick Me Up*, p. 329

HOW THEY MEASURE UP: BIG BUILDINGS

#1: Taipei 101, Taipei, Taiwan, 1,667 ft.

#2: Petronas Towers, Kuala Lumpur, Malaysia, 1,483 ft.

#3: Sears Tower, Chicago, United States, 1,450 ft.

#4: Jin Mao Building, Shanghai, China, 1,381 ft.

#5: CITIC Plaza, Guangzhou, China, 1,283 ft.

– *Pick Me Up*, p. 315

Write your answers in scientific notation.

14. Height of Taipei 101 in feet: _____

15. Height of Sears Tower in inches: _____

16. Height of CITIC Plaza in yards: _____

Activity 5.2: Olympic Ranking
(Informational Trade Book)

Objective: Students will independently or collaboratively devise a system of rankings based on a current math topic (such as decimals, fractions, prime numbers, factors.)

Materials & Preparation:

1. Eastaway, Rob, and Jeremy Wyndham. *Why Do Buses Come in Threes? The Hidden Mathematics of Everyday Life.* New York: John Wiley & Sons, Inc., 1998.

2. Olympic Medal data from past Olympics

Estimated Time: Project varies depending on parameters provided to students

Activity Instructions:

1. To gain an understanding of the context for the next activity, the teacher should first read the excerpt from *Why Do Buses Come In Threes?* titled "Olympic Injustice" on page 97.

2. Review with students how countries are ranked in the Olympics. The goal is to engage students in a discussion about equity in sports rankings as the basis for creating their *own* system of ranking countries participating in the Olympics. (The Olympics provides a simple example as countries are often ranked based only on a tally of medals won.)
   - Should a ranking of countries be based on total number of gold medals? Or total overall medals?
   - Should gold medals factor more into the results than silver or bronze? If so, by how much?
   - Should you base your rankings *only* on medals? What about teams that finished fourth, or fifth?
   - Should their rank in a particular sport "count" the same as another country who may have finished 25th?

3. Now, challenge students to develop a system for ranking the Olympic teams using medal counts/results for various countries in the previous (or current) Olympics. To add interest and sophistication to the activity, provide a variety of math parameters to use as values for their system such as decimals, fractions, prime numbers, and multiples of 3.

Activity 5.2: Olympic Ranking continued

Decimal Example: *All countries start with zero points. For each sport, only teams that win medals earn points. The value for gold, silver, and bronze total " 1 ", therefore gold is worth 0.5 points, silver 0.3 points, and bronze 0.2 points. So, if Canada received a total of 3 silver medals and 2 gold medals, their score is 0.3+ 0.3+ 0.3+ 0.5.+ 0.5 = 1.9. Countries are then ranked based on their total score."*

4. Following the project, read to the class the excerpt from *Why Do Buses Come in Threes* and allow students to share their system of ranking. Compare how the same countries fared within the various systems.

5. A relevant topic is the Bowl Championship Series (BCS) rankings for NCAA college football—a more complicated formula of averages and computer rankings to determine the weekly "Top 25." The system has been fodder for the sports media and fans alike.
    - Should teams be ranked by the total number of games won?
    - Should the team with no losses to "easy" teams rank higher than a team with some losses to "hard" teams?
    - What determines "hard" vs. "easy" teams?

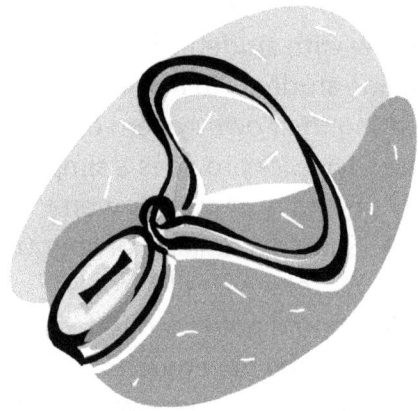

Activity 5.3: Ancestry Arithmetic
(Literature)

Objective: Students will develop an algorithm and practice adding, multiplying, and manipulating fractions while exploring the family tree of the main character in *Artifacts*. Students will personalize by applying the same algorithm to their families.

Materials & Preparation:

1.   Worksheet/pencils

2.   Evans, Mary Anna. *Artifacts*. Scottsdale, AZ: Poisoned Pen Press, 2003

Note: As students will be reading and talking about sections of *Artifacts* during this lesson, students might be interested in checking this book out of the media center.

Estimated Time: 45-60 minutes or homework assignment

Activity Instructions:

1.   Launch: "How many of you have explored your family's genealogy? Do any of you have family members born in countries other than the U.S.? Today we will be exploring the genealogy of Faye Longchamp, a character in *Artifacts*, using fractions to determine the ethnicity of her family members."

2.   Provide students with the Ancestry Arithmetic handout (answers to follow).

Ancestry Arithmetic

Fraction Warm-up:

1. TRUE or FALSE: 1/2 and 2/4 have the same value.

2. TRUE or FALSE: You cannot add fractions unless you have lowest common denominators.

3. When finding a common denominator, you are really finding the denominators':
   a. Greatest Common Factor
   b. Least Common Multiple
   c. Prime Factorization
   d. Square Root

4. TRUE or FALSE: You cannot multiply fractions unless you have common denominators.

ARTIFACTS

In *Artifacts,* the genealogy of Faye Longchamp is revealed through oral history reports and journal entries of long lost relatives. The exploration into one's ancestry often provides information about one's national ethnicity (example: 1/2 Spanish, 1/4 Canadian, 1/4 Chinese). It is a very popular hobby today. People often seek to find from what region of the globe their parents, grandparents, great-grandparents and other family members came from in order to have a better sense of their heritage.

5. Write an algorithm that Faye, or anyone, could use to calculate their ethnicity.

6. From William Whitehall's journal entry on page 15, a daughter Mariah is born to William and Susan. William is European, and Susan is 1/2 Native American and 1/2 European. Use your algorithm in problem #1 to determine the ethnicity of Mariah.

7. Use the information in question 5 to represent Mariah's ethnicity in the circle in Figure 5.1.

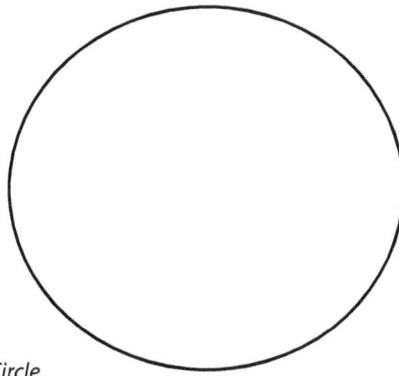

Figure 5.1: Circle

8. If Faye's great-great-great-great-great-grandmother Susan is 1/2 Native American and 1/2 European, this might mean that one of her parents was Native American and one was of European ancestry. Write another combination that could also make her half Native American and half European.

9. Complete your mini-family tree by filling in your parents and grandparents' information. Then use the algorithm in problem #1 to calculate your ethnicity either by continent, country, or state. (Possible examples: 1/2 North American, 1/4 European, 1/4 African *or* 1/4 Portuguese, 1/4 French, 1/4 Japanese *or* 1/2 Texan, 1/4 Floridian, 1/4 Georgian.)

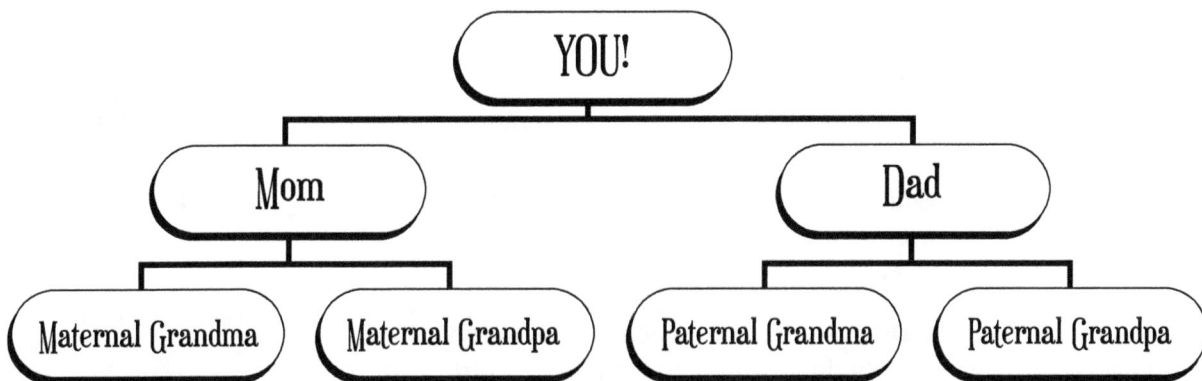

Figure 5.2: Family Tree

10. Use the information in question 9 to represent your ethnicity in the circle below.

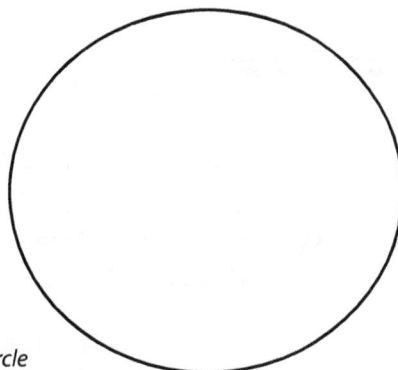

Figure 5.3: Circle

Question 1: TRUE. 1/2 and 2/4 have the same value.

Question 2: FALSE. Utilizing the standard algorithm for adding fractions does require the use of common denominators; however, they do not necessarily need to be the lowest common denominator. Also, it is important to point out that with a clear understanding of fractions one can add a value without finding common denominators. For example, many people can add 1/2 and 1/4 immediately without finding the common denominator.

Question 3: b. When finding lowest common denominators, you are finding the least common multiple.

Question 4: FALSE. You do not need common denominators when multiplying fractions.

Question 5: An algorithm is a series of steps used to solve a problem.
Determine father's ethnicity.
Determine mother's ethnicity.
Child = 1/2 father's ethnicity + 1/2 mother's ethnicity

Question 6:
Mariah = 1/2 (Father) + 1/2 (Mother)
Mariah = 1/2 (William) + 1/2 (Susan)
Mariah = 1/2 European + 1/2 (1/2 Native American + 1/2 European)
Mariah = 1/2 European + 1/4 Native American + 1/4 European
Mariah = 3/4 European + 1/4 Native American

Question 7: See sample representation in Figure 5.4.

Question 8: One other possibility would be if both parents were 1/2 Native American and 1/2 European. There are an infinite number of possible combinations that would yield the same result, but one possibility would be if both of Susan's parents were 1/2 Native American and 1/2 European.

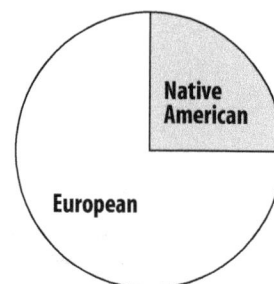

Figure 5.4: Sample Pie Chart

Questions 9 & 10: Students should show lineage back to their grandparents. Students can write "unknown" as this is one distinct possibility. See sample representation in Figure 5.5.

Me = 1/2 Mother + 1/2 Father
Me = 1/2 (1/2 Russian + 1/2 German) + 1/2 British
Me = 1/4 Russian + 1/4 German + 1/2 British

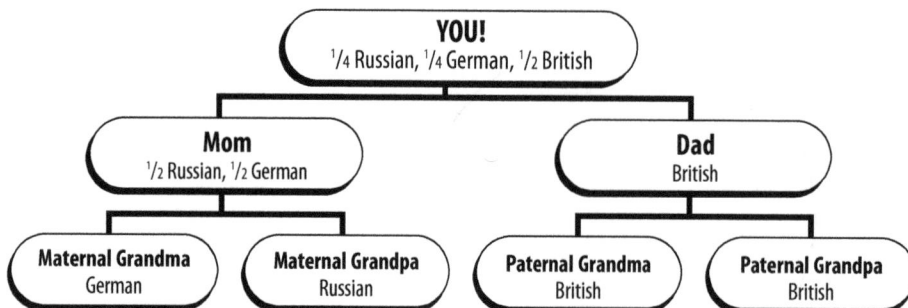

Figure 5.5: Solved Family Tree

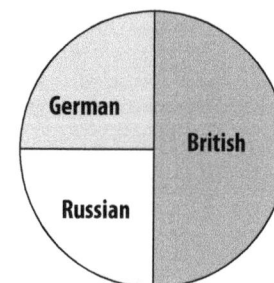

Figure 5.6: Ethnicity Pie Chart

Activity 5.4: No, No, No...
(Environmental Print)

Objective: Students will compare credit offers and determine the amount of tax paid, the monthly payments required, and then create a plan to pay off an item without paying interest. Students will use a formula to calculate compounded interest and evaluate two credit offers.

Materials & Preparation:

1. Worksheet/pencils

2. Students can visit the media center to look up big-ticket items (for example, computer and gaming equipment, furniture) in newspapers or online. Alternatively, Sunday newspapers with their advertising sections can also be used if the media center is unavailable.

Estimated Time: 45 minutes

Vocabulary:

Balance   Interest   Compounded Interest

Activity Instructions:

1. Money lessons compel students to use math in a highly relevant manner—especially when coupled with environmental print sales ads and credit offers. Instead of providing a list of problems to add and multiply involving percents, the context of the problems below requires students to carefully read each question and determine the operation needed. Students also begin to discover how the enticement of "No, No, No" can be misleading if the purchaser does not follow all the terms in the offer. This activity works well in small groups of 2 to 3 students. Following the activity, groups can shop ads for an item, apply sales tax, deduct discounts, and calculate interest compounded for an advertised credit offer. The terms provided are just an example. Most credit offers compound the interest monthly—yearly is provided for ease in calculations. Answers are provided following the student worksheet.

No, No, No...

PICK YOUR OFFER!

NO PAYMENTS FOR 2 YEARS	OR	NO INTEREST FOR 5 YEARS
NO PAYMENTS AND NO INTEREST		NO INTEREST—MONTHLY PAYMENT REQUIRED
NO MINIMUM PURCHASE		NO MINIMUM PURCHASE
NO DOWN PAYMENT		NO DOWN PAYMENT

Figure 5.7: No Payment No Interest

You find an awesome massage chair with a built in MP3 player for $999. Sales tax in your area is 6%. Answer the following questions using the No Payment offer.

1. What is the down payment? _____

2. How many months do you have to pay off the chair with no interest? _____

3. What would the monthly payments need to be to pay off the chair with no interest? _____

Now, recalculate using the No Interest offer. The required monthly payment is $10.

4. What is the down payment? _____

5. How many months do you have to pay off the chair with no interest? _____

6. If you pay the required monthly payment, how much will you have paid in
   5 years? _____

7. If you pay the required monthly payment, what will be the balance in 5 years?

   _____

8. How much MORE do you need to send each month with your required monthly
   payment to pay off the chair with no interest? _____

One of the problems with these offers is despite offering "no payments," if you don't pay off the item by the date advertised, interest is "...compounded annually back to the purchase date at a rate of 23.99%."

To calculate how much interest that will be added, we need a formula:

Balance plus Compounded Interest = Balance * (1 + interest rate) $^{\text{number of years financed}}$

Example: 24% interest after one year:

Balance plus Compounded Interest = 999 * (1+ .24)^1

Balance plus Compounded Interest = 999 * (1.24)^1

Balance plus Compounded Interest = 999 * 1.24

Balance plus Compounded Interest = $1238.76—this is the amount owed after 1 year

9. How much *interest* do I pay if I financed for just 1 year? _____

10. Let's send no payments and choose the No Payment offer.
    Use the formula to complete Table 5.1.

Number of Years	Balance	Compounded Balance	Interest Paid
1	$999	$1238.76	
2	$999		

Table 5.1 2009 Offer

11. What is the total cost of the chair including taxes and interest for the No Payment offer? _____

12. What if I choose the No Interest offer and only send in the monthly required payment? Use the formula to complete Table 5.2.

Number of Years	Starting Amount (Balance in 2012)	Compounded Amount	Interest Paid
5			

Table 5.2 2012 Offer

13. What is the total cost of the chair including taxes and interest for the No Interest offer at the end of the 2 years? _____

14. Compare the two offers. Pick an offer and create a plan for your purchase. Write a few sentences explaining which offer you chose, why, and how much money you will pay each month, if any.

_____

_____

_____

BONUS: There is one consideration to think about—instead of sending money each month to the store, put the money into a bank account or CD and allow it to accrue interest. At the end of the offer pay off the chair to avoid paying interest and keep the amount you earned in the bank.

Your bank offers 4.5% interest compounded *monthly*. The formula for compounding monthly is:

number of
months in bank

Balance plus Compounded Interest = Starting Balance * (1 + (interest rate / 12))

Put the $999 in the bank & determine how much **interest you will earn** on the money after:

2 years: _____ 5 years: _____

No, No, No... Answers

Question 1: The down payment is the sales tax. 999 x .06 = 59.94

Question 2: 2 years = 24 months.

Question 3: 999/24 = ~$41.63

Question 4: The down payment is the sales tax (read the fine print). 999 x .06 = 59.94

Question 5: 5 years = 60 months

Question 6: $10 * 60 = 600

Question 7: The balance would be 999-600 = $399

Question 8: To pay off the amount in 60 months would require a monthly payment of $16.65. Therefore, you would need to send in $16.65 – $10.00 = $6.65; an extra $6.65 each month.

Question 9: I would pay $1,238.76 – $999 = $239.76 in interest

Question 10: See Table 5.3.

Number of Years	Balance	Compounded Balance	Interest Paid
1	$999	$1238.76	$239.76
2	$999	$1536.06	$537.06

Table.5.3 Question 10 Answer

Question 11: Total cost is $999 + $59.94 + $537.06 = $1,596

Question 12: See Table 5.4.

Number of Years	Starting Amount (Balance in 2012)	Compounded Amount	Interest Paid
5	$399	$1169.72	$770.72

Table 5.4 Question 12 Answer

Question 13: Total cost is $999 (chair) + $59.94 (tax) + $770.72 (interest paid) = $1,829.66

or: 600 (monthly payments) + $59.94 (tax) + $1,169.72 (balance owed with interest) = $1,829.66

This is a good opportunity to discuss the downside of paying $1,829.66 for a chair that only cost $999 plus tax five years ago. If you didn't pay the full balance by the end of 5 years, that small $399 balance compounds to $1,169.72, more than the original purchase price. By this time, you probably are ready to buy a new chair rather than pay more for the old one.

Question 14: This question is the starting point for a larger discussion following the activity and the basis for creating a plan for the purchase. Will you choose a plan or just pay cash? If you choose an offer will you send monthly payments? If so, how much?

BONUS: Students should probably use calculators for this section.

Balance plus Compounded Interest = Starting Balance * (1 + (interest rate / 12)) $^{\text{number of months in bank}}$

Two Years

$999 * (1+ (.045/12))^{24}$

$999 * (1+ (.00375))^{24}$

$999 * (1.00375)^{24}$

~$1092.90

Interest earned is $1092.90 ? 999 = ~$93.90

Five Years

$999 * (1+ (.045/12))^{60}$

$999 * (1+ (.00375))^{60}$

$999 * (1.00375)^{60}$

$999 * (1.00375)^{60}$

~$1,250.54

Interest earned is $1,250.54 ? $999 = ~$251.54

Chapter 6

Algebra

Activity 6.1: Crack the Code!
(Informational Trade Book)

Objective: Students will study cryptic messages using two methods: substitution and elimination. Students will encrypt and decrypt messages and find the pattern associated with each system. Students will then create a unique substitution or null cipher system and encrypt a message. Challenge students to crack each other's codes!

Materials & Preparation:

1. Paper

2. Janeczko, Paul B. *Top Secret: A Handbook of Codes, Ciphers, and Secret Writing.* Cambridge, MA: Candlewick Press, 2004.

Note: A class set of *Top Secret* might be useful as students are often interested in cryptic messages and cipher systems.

Estimated Time: 1-2 class periods

Activity 6.1: Crack the Code! continued

Activity Instructions:

1. In algebra, two of the most common methods for solving simultaneous linear equations (or a system of linear equations) are the substitution and elimination methods. As a fun segue into formal introduction of the methods, explore the substitution and elimination ciphers discussed in *Top Secret*. The exploration will provide an algebraic reasoning exercise in using and finding patterns, and allow students to investigate the substitution and elimination concepts in another area.

2. *Top Secret* explains that "codes" replace entire words with symbols, words, or a phrase (think of road signs). A cipher replaces each letter with another letter or symbol. This activity works with ciphers only.

   > "In a substitution cipher, you substitute one symbol for every letter in the plain text. For example, I could substitute the numbers 1 to 26 for the letters of the alphabet. In such a system, HELP would be enciphered as 8-5-12-16."
   >
   > – *Top Secret*, p. 25

3. *Can you think of any other examples of ciphers that you have seen or heard of? Does the cipher involve letters, numbers, or symbols?* Pages 25-51 provide several examples of and practice with substitution ciphers, many of historical note, including: Caesar Cipher (letters), St. Cyr slide (letters), Edgar Allen Poe's use of ciphers in literature (symbols), Morse code (audio or visual symbols), semaphore (visual symbols), and Thomas Jefferson cipher wheel (letters).

4. Arrange for students to work in cooperative pairings. Randomly assign one of the substitution ciphers for your students to explore and work through the practice examples in the book. The students should then create two messages using the cipher method explored: one to encrypt and another to decrypt.

5. Group each of the pairings together into groups of 4 students. Each should share with the other group the substitution cipher method they examined and then challenge the group to encrypt and decrypt their messages using the described method.

   > "One of the basic ways of concealing a message is to use a null cipher. This is a concealment tactic in which only certain letters in a longer message are meaningful. The rest of the letters in the message do a great job of hiding your real message."
   >
   > – *Top Secret*, p. 82

6. Hence, in a null cipher, you need to eliminate unnecessary information to solve the message. The book provides several options for concealing the message such as adding unrelated words and letters.

Activity 6.1: Crack the Code! continued

7. Return students to their original pairings. Provide the examples and practice from pages 82-83. Then allow students to read the letter in *Top Secret* on page 84, "The Cipher That Saved a Life," and its solution on page 85—but do not provide the explanation. Instead ask students to figure out the system (finding the pattern) agreed upon by the captured Sir John to decipher the message.

8. Individually, allow students to create their own system using either the substitution or elimination method and provide an encrypted message for fellow students to decipher within the system they created.

Sample Rubric for Activity:

Cipher Activity	1	2	3
Cipher System	Created a system but did not use substitution or elimination	Created a system using substitution or elimination but it was one already explored previously in the activity	Created a unique system using substitution or elimination
Encrypting	Did not provide an encrypted message	Provided an encrypted message but it was not able to be decrypted using their system	Provided an encrypted message that was able to be decrypted using their system
Decrypting Classmate's Message	Could not decrypt the coded message	Decrypted a portion of the message	Decrypted the message using the classmates system
Creativity & Participation	Limited	Good	Extraordinary

Table 6.1 Sample Rubric

Extension Discussion: Are the symbols used in math, algebra, and computer programming ciphers? Students may even do some research in the media center to prepare for this type of discussion.

Activity 6.2: Tetrahedron
(Literature)

Objective: Students will develop an understanding of algebraic patterns by working with multiple representations: a physical model, a table, and recursive and explicit forms.

Materials & Preparation:

1. Tetrahedron pattern—need at least 16 patterns for each group of students; number of groups of students can vary

2. Worksheet/pencils

3. Scissors and tape

4. Pearsall, Shelley. *All of the Above.* New York: Little, Brown and Company, 2006

Note: As there will be a booktalk of *All of the Above* during this lesson, students may be interested in checking this book out of the media center.

Estimated Time: 45-60 minutes

Vocabulary:

tetrahedron   plural: tetrahedra or tetrahedrons

geometric faces   equilateral triangles

Activity Instructions:

1. This is a hands-on activity based on the project discussed in *All of the Above*—constructing a stage 4 tetrahedron. Students will duplicate the project in the book on a much smaller scale by constructing a stage 1 and 2 tetrahedron. Each level of a tetrahedron increases by a factor of 4—stage 0 (1 tetrahedron), stage 1 (4 tetrahedrons), stage 2 (16 tetrahedrons), and so on. The students will then analyze this pattern to determine how many tetrahedrons, or pieces, would be required to create a tetrahedron of level n by working towards developing recursive and explicit formulas. Students should work in groups of 3-4.

Activity 6.2: Tetrahedron continued

2. Launch: Give a brief booktalk of *All of the Above*. Then conduct a read-aloud by using the following excerpts: pp. 3-4 in which Mr. Collins (the teacher) introduces students to the project of the book and background information; continue with Sharice (pp. 19-26), who provides a better idea of the nature of the project and some information about tools needed to construct a tetrahedron.

Note: This is an excellent book to read in its entirety.

3. Pass out worksheet with tetrahedron template.

4. Conclude the read-aloud by proposing Mr. Collins' math problem on p. 31, which is included on the worksheet. This section provides important information for students by explaining that each level of a tetrahedron increases by a factor of 4. The book uses the term "piece" to describe each tetrahedron: each level is made up of additional tetrahedrons to create a larger tetrahedron.

5. Construct a level 0 tetrahedron. (This would be just 1 piece or 1 tetrahedron). Compare the properties of the tetrahedrons vs. other three-dimensional figures. Students should work together to each create a level 1 tetrahedron on their own so that each group has 4 prepared tetrahedrons altogether.

Answers follow the handout.

Tetrahedron

"Tetra" = 4

"Hedron" =
(Geometric figure with a specified number of faces)

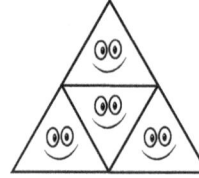

"**Math problem to solve:** Each level of a tetrahedron increases by a factor of four. So, in order to build a bigger tetrahedron, the students at Washington Middle School will need to add a new level and make four times as many pieces. If the California tetrahedron had 4,096 pieces, how many pieces will the Washington Middle School students need to make?"

– Mr. Collins, *All of the Above*, p. 31

1. Answer the question in the box above. _____

2. A stage 0 tetrahedron consists of 1 level and just 1 tetrahedron. How many tetrahedrons will you need to make a *stage 1* tetrahedron? _____

3. Using the tetrahedrons your group has already created, construct a level 1 tetrahedron. Create additional pieces, if necessary.

"Nothing hard about making those little pyramids," Willy Q says, once I show him how you fold three triangles up to a point, glue the sides together, and hold the sides for about a minute until they stick, and you're done."

– Marcel, *All of the Above,* p.183

"An important fact to remember about tetrahedrons: Although the large tetrahedron appears strong and stable, it should be noted that its pieces are joined together only at the smallest of points. The edges and faces are largely separate and unconnected."

– Mr. Collins, *All of the Above*, p. 99

4. How many tetrahedrons will you need to make a *stage 2* tetrahedron? _____

5. Using the tetrahedrons your group has already created, construct a level 2 tetrahedron. Create additional pieces, if necessary.

6. What stage is the California tetrahedron? _____

7. What stage is the Washington Middle School tetrahedron? _____

8. Using the data you found in questions 1-7, complete Table 6.2.

9. Look at the numbers from top to bottom in the "Number of Tetrahedrons" column. What pattern do you notice?

_____

_____

_____

_____

_____

10. If I asked you to find the number of pieces in a stage 10 tetrahedron, what information would you need in order to solve the problem?

_____

_____

_____

Stage	Number of Tetrahedrons
0	1
1	
2	
3	
4	
5	
6	
7	

Table 6.2 Tetrahedron Table

11. If I needed to write a formula to compute the number of tetrahedrons for *any* stage tetrahedron, what would it look like?

_____

_____

12. TRUE or FALSE: "Because of its repeating pattern, the tetrahedron structure can expand to infinity." _____

ULTIMATE BONUS QUESTION: Suppose you wanted to find out how many pieces in a stage 100 tetrahedron. That would take a long time to compute! Look at the numbers from left to right in the table. How does the stage number and the number of tetrahedrons relate? Find the pattern and you can find the number of pieces for *any* stage tetrahedron easily.

Tetrahedron

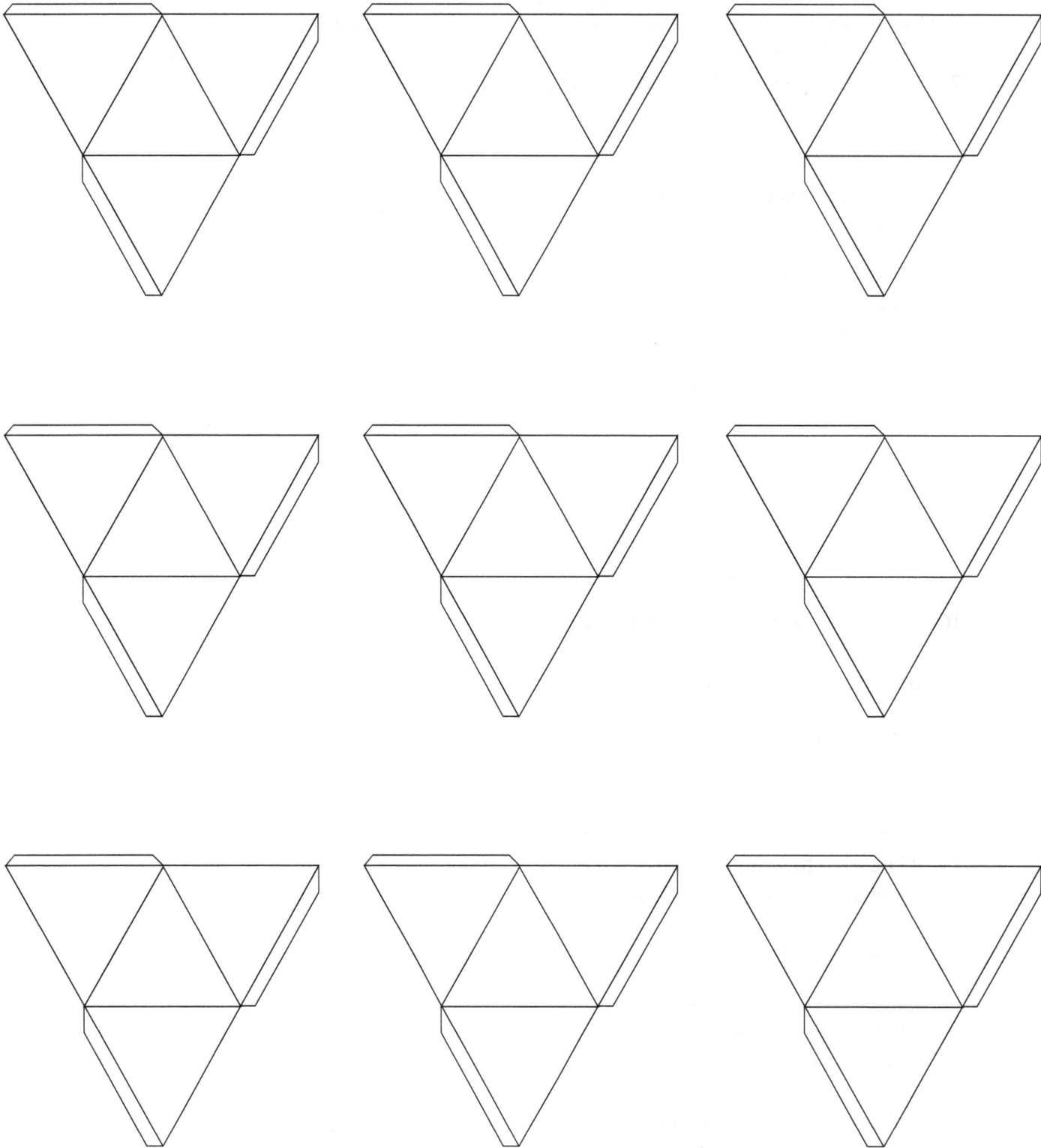

Figure 6.1 Tetrahedrons

Tetrahedron Answers

Question 1: Washington Middle School students need to make 4,096 * 4 = 16,384 pieces, tetrahedrons

Questions 2 & 3: Since each level increases by a factor of 4, a stage 1 tetrahedron would be 1*4, or 4 pieces. Notice the instructions do not dictate to place three pieces on the bottom and one on top. Allow students time to experiment with the four pieces to see if they can determine their proper placement. Remind students the overall shape will still remain the same as a level 0 tetrahedron. [See sample rubric.]

Questions 4 & 5: Since each level increases by a factor of 4, a stage 2 tetrahedron would be 4*4, or 16 pieces. Again, allow students time to experiment with the pieces to see if they can determine the proper placement. Remind students the overall shape will still remain the same as a level 0 and level 1 tetrahedron. The placement of the pieces should be as follows: create four level 1 tetrahedrons, place three level 1 tetrahedrons on the bottom, and one level 1 tetrahedron on top. [See sample rubric.] Table 6.3 is a sample rubric for construction of level 1 and level 2 tetrahedrons.

Stage 1/Stage 2 Tetrahedron	1	2	3
Number of Pieces	Did not know how to work problem	Calculated, but incorrect	Correct
Individual Pieces	Pieces were made incorrectly	Pieces were made correctly, but not of good quality	Pieces were made correctly, of good quality and uniformity
Design	Placement of pieces was incorrect and/or could not create the level tetrahedron requested	Placement of pieces to create the level of tetrahedron was almost correct with only slight modifications needed	Placement of pieces to create the level of tetrahedron was done correctly
Collaboration	Group was not able to work together effectively	Group worked well together	Group demonstrated an outstanding ability to work collaboratively

Table 6.3 Tetrahedron Sample Rubric

Questions 6 & 7: This problem is working in reverse of the previous problems. Now students are given a number of pieces and asked to determine the level. If a stage 2 = 16 pieces, then stage 3 is 16*4, or 64 pieces. Stage 4 is 64 *4, or 256. Stage 5 is 256*4, or 1,024. Stage 6 is 1,024*4 or 4,096 the size of the California tetrahedron. Therefore, stage 7 is 4,096*4, or 16,384—the size of the Washington Middle School students' tetrahedron.

Questions 8 -11: The table should be completed as shown in Table 6.4. As you move down the column from 1 to 16,384 the number of tetrahedrons in the previous stage multiplied by 4 gives you the number of pieces needed for the next stage. This is information given at the outset, but now students see it in context. This a sequence—to find the number of pieces in a stage 10 tetrahedron, you would need to know the number of pieces in a stage 9 tetrahedron and then multiply the value by 4. This is an example of a recursive, or iterative relation, since you can determine the number of tetrahedrons required by looking back at the previous level. Formally written in recursive form:

$$t_0 = 1 \; ; t_n = t_{(n-1)} \cdot 4$$

Stage	Number of Tetrahedrons
0	1
1	9
2	16
3	64
4	256
5	1024
6	4096
7	16,384

Table 6.4 Questions 8-11 Answer

NCTM suggests the use of "NEXT" and "NOW" to help students understand the process. If you NOW are on stage 1, and want to know stage 2, the NEXT stage:

$$NOW = 1 \; ; NEXT = NOW \cdot 4$$

Another notation used as a precursor to the more formal notation is "START, NEXT, CURRENT."

$$START = 1 \; ; NEXT = CURRENT \cdot 4$$

Real-world application: All of the notation shown in Questions 8-11 is reminiscent of computer programming code.

Question 12: TRUE. Mr. Collins on p. 226 "One final fact to remember about tetrahedrons: Because of its repeating pattern, the tetrahedron structure can expand to infinity. So, in theory, you can keep adding more and more tetrahedrons forever..."

Question 13: ULTIMATE BONUS QUESTION. The number of tetrahedrons is equal to "4" raised to the stage number. Stage 0 = 4^0, or 1 Stage 1 = 4^1, or 4 Stage 2 = 4^2, or 16, etc.

This can be written explicitly as: stage $n = 4^n$

Extension: Graph the values in the table as x (stage number) and y (number of tetrahedron) on graph paper or using a graphing calculator. Is the relationship linear? Ex. $y = 4^x$

Discuss the information as a function: $f(x) = 4^x$

Research Waclaw Sierpinski and his work with fractal geometry in the media center. Google "Sierpinski Tetrahedron" and see images of tetrahedron constructed by other students.

Activity 6.3: Decisions, Decisions, Decisions . . . (Environmental Print)

Objective: Students will represent and analyze functions in various forms including tables, graphs, and equations, and find a real-world model to represent in a form of their choosing.

Materials & Preparation:

1. Sample environmental print
2. Worksheet
3. Party paper/tracing paper

Estimated Time: 2 class periods

Activity Instructions:

In this activity, students explore options in DVD rentals and represent the situation as a function in a variety of ways, but we use a fictional company to frame the work. Suggested questions are provided in italics. Students are challenged to find another model in their environment to represent as a function. We present the lesson and answers here prior to the student handout for clarity due to the complexity of the activity.

Prior to the activity, find an example of environmental print similar to the one shown on the worksheet. Read the text aloud to students and question for understanding. *Have you seen offers similar to this? What information is important? How do you determine which plan is better?*

Students should complete the table as shown in Table 6.5.

# of DVDs/month	Total monthly cost: MOVIE BUFF member	Total monthly cost: non-member
1	$(15.00) + 1 * 1.00 = 16.00$	4.75
2	15+2=17	9.50
3	15+3=18	14.25
4	15+4=19	19.00
5	15+5=20	23.75

Table 6.5 Movie Buff Table

Questions 1-3: One DVD per month would cost 15.00 + 1.00 = $16.00 as a MOVIE BUFF member and $4.75 as a non-member. Therefore, you should not join the club because it costs more to rent the DVD as a member than a non-member. These two values $16.00 and $4.75 are the cost/rental.

Questions 5-6: Five DVDs per month would cost 15.00 + 5.00 = $20.00 as a MOVIE BUFF member, and 4.75*5.00 = $23.75 as a non-member. Therefore, you should join the club because at 5 rentals/month it costs less to rent the DVDs as a member than a non-member. *What is the cost/rental for each option? For each option, what happens to the cost/rental as the number of DVD rentals increases?*

Activity 6.3: Decisions, Decisions, Decisions. . . continued

Question 7: You would need to rent 5 DVDs each month to make joining the MOVIE BUFF club a better value over being a non-member.

Question 8: At 4 DVD rentals there is no cost difference between membership and non-membership.

The two graphs should look similar to the graphs shown in Figure 6.2.

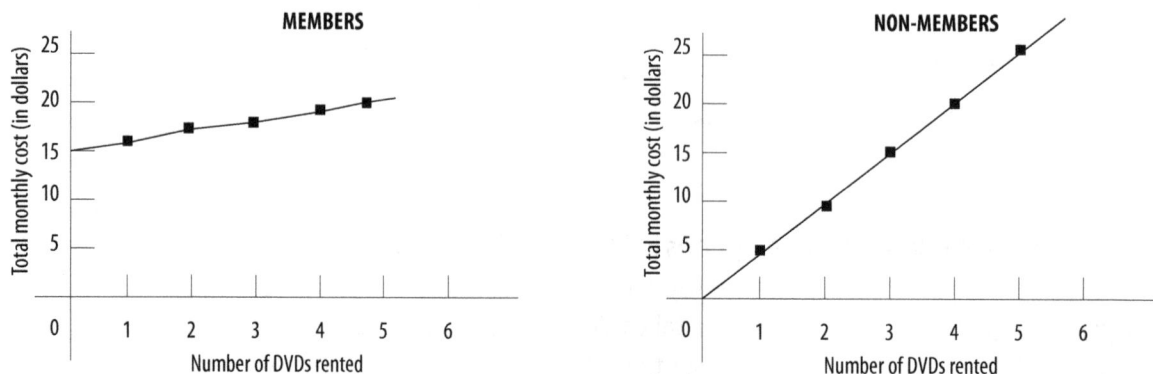

When overlaid, the graph should look like:

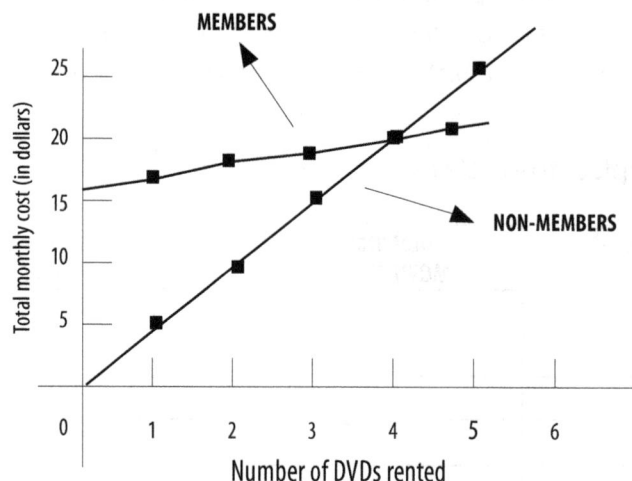

Figure 6.2 Graphs

The lines intersect at 4 DVD rentals since they both would cost $19.00. *Is the graph linear? How would you describe the slope in the two graphs you created? In this graph, what does the slope represent? (cost/rental) Are the lines in the graph increasing?* Allow students time to analyze the graph and see the relationship revealed earlier in the table. Students should find that when renting <4 DVDs non-membership is the better value, when renting >4 DVDs membership is the better value, and at 4 rentals the cost is the same.

Question 13: Sample equations for each of the graphs:

monthly costs = 15.00 + (1• # of rentals) and monthly costs = 4.75 • # of rentals

OR

y = 15.00 + 1x , or y = 15.00 + x and y = 0 + 4.75x, or y = 4.75x

Activity 6.3: Decisions, Decisions, Decisions. . . continued

Question 14: When x is equal to 4 both equations result in $19.00 for y.

Questions 15-16: The value of x equal to zero means "no DVDs were rented." The value of y equal to zero can only occur when non-members rent no DVDs. Even if members rent no DVDs, their monthly cost will start at $15.00 and therefore can never equal zero.

What is a function? Before students begin the challenge to find other examples in their world that can be represented as a function, assess students' understanding of the concept of "function" by allowing students to describe the relationship modeled in the table, graph, and equation. *What is a variable? What is the independent variable? What is the dependent variable?* As a member or non-member, the monthly cost for DVD rentals is a function of number of DVDs rented. Use the original example read prior to the activity as another source of information to further the discussion.

Challenge students to find other examples of environmental print that can be represented as a function. Allow a class period for students to read the examples found and continue to develop a deeper understanding of functions and their application in the real world. Simple examples include season passes to theme parks (how many visits do you need to make to break even?) and warehouse clubs (how much do you need to spend before you recoup the membership fee?). More complex examples include Napster, Netflix, Blockbuster, and GameFly subscriptions and cell phone plans wherein there are often several tiers of service provided. Students can work through these and other problems in the media center with Internet connections.

Decisions, Decisions, Decisions. . .

A movie rental store offers a MOVIE BUFF club membership: pay a monthly fee of $15.00 and rent all the DVDs you want for $1 each. Non-members pay $4.75 per DVD rental.

Based on this information, create a table comparing the monthly costs of renting movies as a member and a non-member.

# of DVDs/month	Total monthly cost: MOVIE BUFF member	Total monthly cost: non-member
1	16.00	4.75
2		
3		
4		
5		

Figure 6.3 DVD Chart

1. How much would it cost to rent 1 DVD per month as a MOVIE BUFF member?

2. How much would it cost to rent 1 DVD per month as a non-member?

3. If you rent 1 DVD per month, should you join the MOVIE BUFF club? Why or why not?

4. How much would it cost to rent 5 DVDs per month as a MOVIE BUFF club member?

5. How much would it cost to rent 5 DVDs per month as a non- member?

6. If you rent 5 DVDs per month, should you join the MOVIE BUFF club? Why or why not?

7. How many DVDs would you need to rent each month to make joining the MOVIE BUFF club a better value over being a non-member?

8. If you joined the MOVIE BUFF club, how many DVDs do you need to rent to break even?

9. Trace the following graph onto tracing paper.

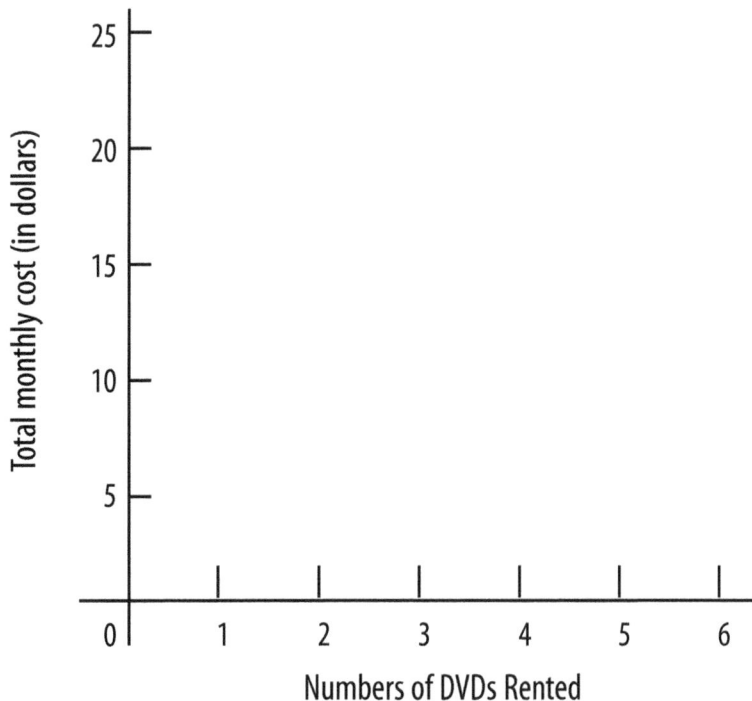

Figure 6.4 DVD Rental Chart

10. Complete the graph in Figure 6.4 using the 5 values of **total monthly costs for a MOVIE BUFF member.**

11. Complete the 2nd graph (the one you traced) using the 5 values of **total monthly costs for non-members.**

12. Overlay the tracing paper onto the other graph. Where do the lines intersect?

13. Write two equations, one for each of the graphs you created.

14. For what value of *x* would both equations result in the same *y?*

15. Can the value of *x* be equal to zero?

16. When can the value of *y* be equal to zero?

Challenge: Find another example in your environment of a relationship that can be represented as a function to share with the class. Think about places you visit online, recent purchases you have made, and stores you often shop. Print out or pick up the information to share with the class.

Chapter 7

Geometry

Activity 7.1: Crafty Geometry
(Informational Text)

Objective: Students will use hands-on activities to explore an array of geometry topics.

Materials & Preparation:

1. See individual activities.

Estimated Time: varies, most involve 1 class period/activity

Activity Instructions:

We have provided a series of kinesthetic activities from a variety of informational texts exploring familiar geometry topics including: 3-dimensional figures and polygons, cross-sections, tessellation, and transformations. Multiple copies of these books will facilitate a smoother rotation of activities. Through crafts like painting and origami, students will enjoy the process and the end-result, while the math is integrated into the activity seamlessly.

Constructing Domes

Gumdrop Dome

Materials: toothpicks and gumdrops
Source: Editors of *YES Mag. Fantastic Feats and Failures*. Tonawanda, NY: Kids Can Press, 2004, p. 9.
This simple project results in a geodesic dome with a pentagon base.

Dome, Sweet Dome

Materials: newspaper, broom, tape, yard stick, scissors, marker, stapler
Source: Wyatt, Valerie, and Pat Cupples. *The Math Book for Girls and Other Beings Who Count.* Niagara Falls, NY: Kids Can Press, 2000, pp. 26-27.
A unique and complex model is described. The text provides instructions for creating a geodesic dome with a decagon base out of newspaper tubes.

Ripping Angles

Materials: paper, ruler
Source: Ball, Johnny. *Go Figure! A Totally Cool Book about Numbers*. New York: DK Publishing, 2005, pp. 52 and 54.
Go Figure provides a visual activity to prove the three angles in a triangle equal 180° and the four angles in a quadrilateral equal 360°.

Creating Polyhedra

Envelope Tetrahedron

Materials: envelope, scissors
Source: Ball, Johnny. *Go Figure! A Totally Cool Book about Numbers*. New York: DK Publishing, 2005, pp. 60-61.
Step-by-step instructions allow students to create a tetrahedron from an ordinary envelope. More advanced designs are offered for other 3-dimensional shapes including an icosahedron and dodecahedron.

Money Polyhedra

Materials: dollar bill (real or fake)
Source: Montroll, John. *Dollar Bill Origami*. Canada: General Publishing Company, LTD., 2003, pp. 34-41.
Detailed fold-by-fold directions for three origami designs: tetrahedron, cube, and diamond, each from an ordinary dollar bill. Page 10 provides dimensions, angle measures, and ratios to create dollar bill sized paper from a square.

Activity 6.3: Decisions, Decisions, Decisions. . . continued

Paper Cubes

Materials: paper, index card, scissors, tape, compass, ruler, glue
Source: Ross, Catherine Sheldrick. *Squares: Shapes in Math, Science, and Nature*. New York: Kids Can Press, 1996, p. 45-51.

Students determine how many squares are needed to construct a 3-dimensional cube from a 2-dimensional sheet of paper. Students can also design a cube net and then construct the cube. More advanced shape designs are also provided including triangular prisms, square based pyramids, cuboctahedron, and rhombicuboctahedrons! (pp. 50-51).

Straw Cubes

Materials: straws, paper clips, pins
Source: Ross, Catherine Sheldrick. *Squares: Shapes in Math, Science, and Nature*. New York: Kids Can Press, 1996, pp. 52-53.

Students construct a prism using straws and paper clips and discover how the use of triangles can add rigidity to the structure.

Bubble Cubes

Materials: wire, wire cutters, cardboard, scissors, ruler, pencil, compass, jar, bubbles
Source: Ross, Catherine Sheldrick. *Squares: Shapes in Math, Science, and Nature*. New York: Kids Can Press, 1996, p. 58-59.

Think all bubbles are spheres? In this activity, students blow cube-shaped bubbles from a wire frame.

Paradox Cubes

Materials: 3" sticky notes; need 21
Source: Mitchell, David. *Sticky Note Origami: 25 Designs to Make at Your Desk*. London: PRC Publishing, 2005, pp. 54-57.

While not completely cubes, this paradoxical pattern of cube tiles "resembles Escher's famous impossible figure drawings."

Collapsible Cube

Materials: 3" sticky notes; need 8
Source: Mitchell, David. *Sticky Note Origami: 25 Designs to Make at Your Desk*. London: PRC Publishing, 2005, pp. 120-127.

This complicated and fun design is included for its use of Silver Rectangles (rectangles with sides in the ratio 1:). Who knew paper folding was so mathematical?

Netting

Materials: pencil, paper, scissors, tape
Source: Wyatt, Valerie and Pat Cupples. *The Math Book for Girls and Other Beings Who Count*. Niagara Falls, NY: Kids Can Press, 2000, pp. 18-19.

Transform 2-dimensional paper into 3-dimensional tetrahedrons, hexahedrons (cubes), octahedrons, and dodecahedrons with printed net templates.

Experimenting with Tessellation

Cairo Tessellation

Materials: 3" sticky notes
Source: Mitchell, David. *Sticky Note Origami: 25 Designs to Make at Your Desk.* London: PRC Publishing, 2005, pp. 58-61.
The "Cairo Tessellation is an attractive and intriguing pattern," frequently used in Islamic design, is created by tessellating irregular pentagon tiles. Tiles can be combined as a simple irregular hexagon or in more complex ways. Contrasting color sticky notes add effect.

Tessellating Wrapping Paper

Materials: tracing paper, pencil, scissors, sponges, paint, paper
Source: Wyatt, Valerie and Pat Cupples. *The Math Book for Girls and Other Beings Who Count.* Niagara Falls, NY: Kids Can Press, 2000, pp. 34-35.
This simple activity allows students to experiment with patterns by combining triangular and pentagonal shaped sponge prints to create a tessellation with paint.

Tessellating and Transforming Wrapping Paper

Materials: paper, cardboard, pencil, ruler, square, scissors, glue
Source: Ross, Catherine Sheldrick. *Squares: Shapes in Math, Science, and Nature.* New York: Kids Can Press, 1996, pp. 34-35.
In this activity, students use right triangle cardboard stamps to create a tessellation with paint. The movement of the triangle across the paper provides discussion for transformations such as rotation and translation.

Folding Geometric Shapes

Materials: 1.5" 2" sticky notes
Source: Mitchell, David. *Sticky Note Origami: 25 Designs to Make at Your Desk.* London: PRC Publishing, 2005, pp. 67-74.
Students will have fun creating two octagonal shapes: a ring and star. The octagonal ring is composed of both an octagonal ring and hole in the center. The final product reveals an interesting pattern when held up to the light. The eight-pointed star has an octagonal hole in the center.

Cutting Cones

Materials: modeling clay/dough, dental floss or plastic knives
Source: Ball, Johnny. *Go Figure! A Totally Cool Book about Numbers.* New York: DK Publishing, 2005, pp. 64.
Students make cuts through the cone to examine the cross section. The described activity creates four curves: circle, ellipse, parabola, and hyperbola.

Activity 7.2: Angle of Guilt
(Literature)

Objective: Students will use ballistic evidence presented in the story to draw a diagram and determine the trajectory of the bullet to solve a crime. Students will use their diagram, additional information, and properties of similar figures to answer additional questions related to the story.

Materials & Preparation:

1. Brown, Jeremy. *Crime Files: Four Minute Forensic Mysteries: Shadow of Doubt.* New York: Scholastic, 2006. For this activity students will read the short story "The Angle of Guilt," pp.169-172, so you will need multiple copies.

2. Worksheet/pencils

3. Straight edge

Estimated Time: 45-60 minutes

Activity Instructions:

Again, we provide detailed directions and answers prior to the student worksheet because of the complexity of the activity.

Write instructions for the reading on a transparency or on the board: *Ask students to circle unknown words as they read, and underline words that they think are possible clues or helpful information.*

1. Read "The Angle of Guilt" aloud to the class.

2. Question students: "What words did we circle?" *Help students define unknown words by eliciting information from the class.* "What words did we underline?" *Students should offer the height of the entrance and exit holes on the refrigerator.*

3. Provide students with the worksheet. Drawing pictures is an excellent way for students to solve problems involving similar figures.

4. Students should label the refrigerator as indicated in the diagram. (The story does not specify if the referenced "left side" is when facing the front or the rear of the refrigerator. As such, some may label the entrance and exit hole in reversed positions. Both perspectives would be correct.)

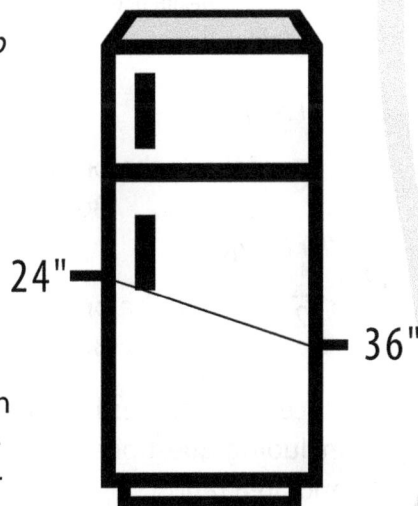

Figure 7.1 Refrigerator 1

Activity 7.2: Angle of Guilt continued

5. The line drawn to connect the points illustrates the rod inserted by the investigators in the story, a straight line. (This would not be the actual trajectory of a bullet since the path of a projectile is curved.) The diagram provides a visual for the solution on p. 172 in the story. The angle of trajectory is acute. To determine the distance the bullet descended along its path through the refrigerator, students should subtract the exit height of 24 inches from the entrance height of 36 inches and obtain 12 inches. This provides one key side measurement for solving the remaining questions.

6. Despite the variations in width, the entrance hole for all three refrigerators would be 36 inches. However, the height of the exit holes would differ. To determine the height of the exit holes for the other sized refrigerators, students need to set up a proportion. The width of the refrigerator and the distance the bullet descends provides the required information for the proportion.

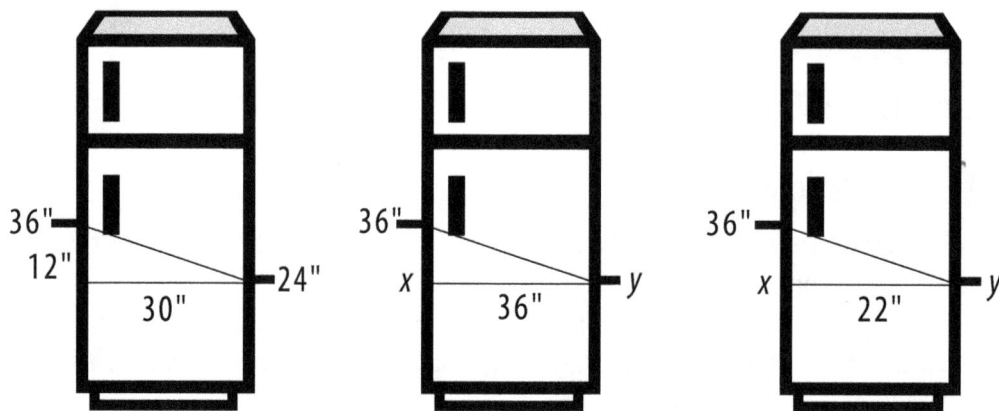

x = the distance the bullet descends y = the height of the exit hole
Height of exit hole = height of entrance hole – the distance the bullet descends

Figure 7.2 Refrigerators

Larger Fridge:
$\frac{12}{30} = \frac{?}{36}$ Solving the proportion: (12*36) / 30 = 14.4 Therefore, x = 14.4 inches.
36 – 14.4 = 21.6 Therefore, y = 21.6 inches.

Smaller Fridge:
$\frac{12}{30} = \frac{?}{22}$ Solving the proportion: (12*22) / 30 = 8.8 Therefore, x = 8.8 inches.
36 – 8.8= 27.2 Therefore, y = 27.2 inches.

7. Once the triangles have been labeled on the diagrams, extend the discussion by including questions about the corresponding angles in the triangles, and perimeter and area ratios.

Other extensions: Introduce the Pythagorean Theorem to calculate the length of the hypotenuse in all three triangles. Use of trigonometric functions is an alternate method for determining missing side lengths and angle measurements.

52   *Teaching Mathematics through Reading: Methods and Materials for Grades 6-8*

The Angle of Guilt

1. Using the evidence in "The Angle of Guilt," label the diagram of the refrigerator with the bullet entrance and exit holes and their distances from the floor.

2. Use a straight edge to connect the entrance and exit holes, drawing the rod inserted by the investigators in the story.

3. "Why did Burton suspect the man on the second floor?"

   _____

   _____

   _____

   _____

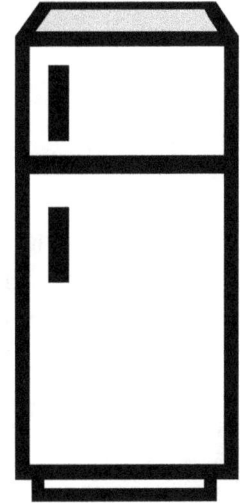

Figure 7.3 Refrigerator

4. Is the angle of trajectory acute, obtuse, right, or straight? _____

5. A bullet descends as it travels along its path. How many inches did the bullet descend from the time it entered the refrigerator until it exited? _____

6. Suppose the refrigerator in the story is 30" wide. Similar refrigerators are 36" and 22" wide. Assuming the other refrigerators are placed in the same location as the 30" wide refrigerator, what do you think would be the height of the ENTRANCE hole in both the larger and smaller refrigerators?

   _____

7. Use what you know about similar figures to determine the height of the EXIT hole in the larger and smaller refrigerators. Label the diagram of the refrigerators below and show all calculations.

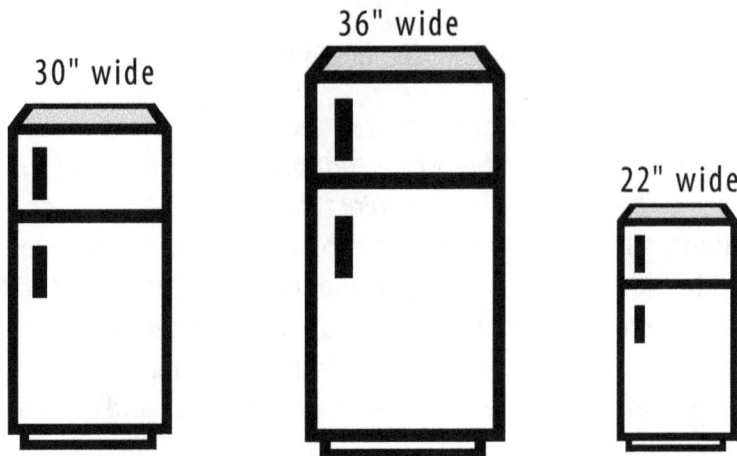

36" wide

30" wide

22" wide

Figure 7.4 Refrigerators 2

24"

Height of exit hole: _____   Height of exit hole: _____   Height of exit hole: _____

Activity 7.3: Number Prefixes
(Environmental Print)

Objective: Students will explore deconstructing words into prefixes, suffixes, and stems to determine the meaning of unknown words and learn number prefixes commonly used in naming polygons and their application in other words.

Materials & Preparation:

Slides or overheads with the suggested slides/transparencies

Estimated Time: 45-60 minutes

Activity Instructions:

1. Use this lesson to introduce and reinforce the power of breaking up unknown words into their linguistic parts. The vocabulary in mathematics can be especially relevant in other areas of the English language. For example, an understanding of number prefixes can help students readily define geometric terms and provides a basis for learning interdisciplinary vocabulary.

2. Show slide. Most students will know of the word "phobia" meaning "fear of something." Allow time for students to provide examples of known words with the root "phobia" (e.g., arachnophobia.) *If you know what "phobia" means, what do you think the prefix "arachno-" means? (spider) What is an arachnid? (spider) What is arachnoloy? (study of spiders) What do you think the suffix "−ology" means? (study of).* Continue to show examples of how deconstructing one word helps to understand the meaning of another one.

What do you think this word means?
PHOBIA
Where have you heard it before?

3. Show next slide. "Technophobia" is fear of technology/computers. *Did you determine the meaning based on other words that begin with "techno-" such as technology? Hey, there's the suffix "−ology" again!* "Photophobia" is fear of light/strong light. If students suggest "fear of taking a picture," provide other examples of words with the same prefix, and help students to find "light" as the commonality. *(e.g., Photosynthesis, photograph). What other words begin with "photo-" that we can use to help us find the meaning?* "Aerophobia" is a fear of flying. Words with the same prefix include aerodynamics, aeronautics and aerobatics.

Activity 7.3: Number Prefixes continued

Now, what do you think these words mean?
> Technophobia
> Photophobia
> Aerophobia

How do you think you would say these words?

+phobia

4. Show next slide. Elicit information from students about known parts of the words: "tri-"and "deka-" are possible examples. If students have difficulty, you can start with "Triskaidekaphobia," the fear of the number thirteen. (On Friday the 13th, I have been known to put on my board: "Do you have paraskevidekatriaphobia?" Students are intrigued by the length of the word and want to figure out its meaning. Many students want to write it down to repeat at home for friends and parents!) Pronounced: (para skee vee deck uh tree uh phobia).

> Here's a tough one!
> Paraskevidekatriaphobia
> Do YOU have it?
>
> p a r a s k e v i d e k a t r i a p h o b i a
> Friday 13 fear of

Literature extension: Read an excerpt from The Midnighters series (see Chapter 2) wherein the number thirteen is a source of protection against the darklings.

5. Next slide. "Octagon" is an eight-sided polygon. "Oct-" means "eight" and "-gon" is a closed-plane figure. Knowing this, how many legs does an octopus have? An octave is a musical interval; how many notes do you think are in an octave?

> What is an Octagon?
> What does "oct-" mean?
> What does "-gon" mean?

Research extension: Why is October the 10th month, and not the 8th?

6. Repeat for the prefixes in Table 7.1

Prefix	Meaning	Sample Words
uni and mono	one	unicycle, unite, unicorn, monocle, monopoly, monotone
bi and di	two	bicycle, bifocal, binary, bikini, divide, diagonal
tri	three	tricycle, trident, triple, triangle
tetra and quad	four	tetrahedron, tetrapod, tetragon, quadrilateral, quadruple, quadriceps
pent and quint	five	pentagon, pentacle, quintuplet, quintillion
hex and sex	six	hexagon, sexagenarian, sextuplet, sextant
septa and hepta	seven	septillion, septennial, heptagon, heptarchy
non	nine	nonillion, nonagon
dec	ten	decameter, decathlon, decade

Table 7.1 Prefixes

Activity 7.4: Alphabet Soup Symmetry & Transformations (Environmental Print)

Objective: Students will analyze uppercase and lowercase letters and numbers to find those characters with rotational and line symmetry. Students will also determine the effects of rotations and reflections on characters

Materials & Preparation: Worksheet

Estimated Time: 45-60 minutes

Activity Instructions:

1. Letters and numbers are everywhere in our environment. This is a good visualization activity for assessing both rotational and line symmetry in commonly seen characters.

Note: the font used is important as other representations of the characters can provide different results. For example, showing the number one as "1" vs. "l" affects its symmetry. This could also be a source of discussion.

2. Rotational Symmetry: All of the letters and numbers below when rotated less than 360° line up again with the original image.

HINOSXZ   losxz   l O

Figure 7.5 Rotational Symmetry 1

3. Line Symmetry: E and K are very close possibilities, however there is slightly more space on the lower half than the top half. The letter O has an infinite number of lines of symmetry, the number 0 is slightly oval so there are only 2.

Extension: Have students draw the lines of symmetry as shown in Figure 7.6.

4. When rotated 180° the "M" becomes "W." The reflection of "b" is "d," and the reflection of "q" is "p." When rotated 180° the "b" becomes "q," and "p" becomes "d."

5. Answers to Activity Questions 12 & 13—TRUE: All of the letters when translated remain the same as their original image (pre-image); FALSE: As stated in question 3, the letter O has an infinite number of lines of symmetry.

A B C D H I M O T U V W X Y
a c i l o t u v w x

Figure 7.6 Line Symmetry 1

Alphabet Soup Symmetry and Transformations

ABCDEFGHIJKLMNOPQRSTUVWXYZ

Figure 7.7 Rotational Symmetry 2

1. Find **7** letters in Figure 7.7 that have rotational symmetry.

2. Find the **12** letters in Figure 7.7 that have line symmetry.

3. Rotate **M** 180°. What letter do you get? _____

a b c d e f g h i j k l m n o p q r s t u v w x y z

Figure 7.8 Rotational Symmetry 3

4. Find **5** letters above that have rotational symmetry:

5. Find **10** letters above that have line symmetry:

6. What letter is the reflection of **b:** _____

7. What letter is the reflection of **q:** _____

8. Rotate **b** 180°. What letter do you get? _____

9. Rotate **p** 180°. What letter do you get? _____

1 2 3 4 5 6 7 8 9 0

Figure 7.9 Rotational Symmetry 4

10. Find a number in Figure 7.9 that has rotational symmetry:

11. Find a number in Figure 7.9 that has line symmetry:

12. TRUE or FALSE: All of the letters when translated remain the same as the original image. _____

13. TRUE or FALSE: The letter O has 2 lines of symmetry. _____

Chapter 8

Measurement

Activity 8.1: It's All Relative. . .

Objective : Students will calculate the ratio of 2 images and find the scale factor of the images and the actual size.

Materials & Preparation:

1. Worksheet, pencils, and rulers.

2. Harris, Nicholas, and Sebastian Quigley. *How Big Are They?* Baltimore, MD: Flying Frog Publishing/Allied Publishing, 2004.

Estimated Time: 30 minutes

Activity Instructions:

Often ratio problems pose questions similar to this: "What is the ratio of boys to girls...or red marbles to green marbles?" Less frequently, ratio in measurements is seen. As a foundation to future lessons in dilation, activities involving size and scaling are important concepts to recognize. This lesson surrounds the reading of the informational trade book *How Big Are They?* This is a picture book.

Activity 8.1: It's All Relative. . .continued

The answers listed correspond with the attached worksheet.

Questions 1 & 2: The ratio is 20/28, simplified to 4/7. This can also be written as 4 to 7 or 4:7.

Question 3: The domestic cat and magpie have a ratio of 1 to 1.

Question 4: The ratio is 20 to 482, simplified to 10:241.

Questions 5 & 6: In these questions, students need to realize the two items are *not* in the same units. The ratio is not 20 to 30 since one is in inches and the other is in feet. To show the correct ratio, both items should be represented in inches or both in feet. In inches, the ratio is 20:360, simplified to 1:18. Students should see and translate that information into an understanding that it would take 18 magpies to equal the length of just one triceratops.

Questions 7 & 8: In these questions, students work with decimals and ratios. The ratio is 0.14 to 0.02, simplified to 7:1. Students should see that it would take 7 grains of sand to equal 1 yellow ant.

Question 9: "General Sherman's" height to width ratio is: 275 to 36.

Question 10: 482 x 12 = 5784 / 28 = about 206 babies

Question 11: 12385/482 = about 26 Great Pyramids

Question 12: Answers will vary depending on the student's height. Ex. 5' tall student, 5:394

Questions 13 & 14: The ratio is 3:10, so the scale factor is 3/10 or .3.

Questions 15 & 16: The ratio is 3:1.5, so the scale factor is 2.

Questions 17 - 19: A scale factor less than 1 would mean the drawing is smaller than the actual object. A scale factor greater than 1 would mean the drawing is larger than the actual object. A scale factor of 1 means the image and the actual object are the same size.

Extension Activity: Have students create their own page in *How Big Are They* by using grid paper, selecting the scale for each grid square, and selecting a group of items to represent as scale drawings. (Examples: family members including pets, their bedroom furniture, and so on.)

It's All Relative...

After reading *How Big Are They,* do you feel small? The scale drawings in the book provide a powerful perspective of how big and small things really are. But what if you weren't able to create all the pictures in the book? Is there another way to show the relationship between two of the people, places, or things shown in the book? *Yes*—you can use *numbers* to illustrate the relationship by using *ratios.*

RATIOS: Use the information in your book to find the ratio between the items in each question.

1. What is the ratio of the length of the domestic cat to the 6-month-old baby? _____

2. Show the ratio from question 1 in another form: _____

3. What is the ratio of the length of the domestic cat to the magpie? _____

4. What is the ratio of the height of the dump truck to the Great Pyramid? _____

5. What is the ratio of the length of the magpie to the triceratops? _____

6. How many magpies would you need to equal the length of one triceratops? _____

7. What is the ratio of the yellow ant to the grain of sand? _____

8. How many grains of sand would you need to equal the size of one yellow ant? _____

9. What is the ratio of "General Sherman's" length to width? _____

10. About how many 6-month-old babies would you need to stack to reach the top of the Great Pyramid? _____

11. About how many Great Pyramids would you need to stack up to reach the top Mount Fuji? _____

12. What is the ratio of *your* height to the Ushiku Amida Buddha? _____

SCALE FACTOR: Find the scale factor of the items in each question.

13. Measure the height of a grid square on pages 12-13. What is the ratio of the actual height of each square to its represented height? _____

14. What is the scale factor for pages 12-13? _____

15. Measure the height of a grid square on pages 10-11. What is the ratio of the actual height of each square to its represented height? _____

16. What is the scale factor for pages 10-11? _____

17. A scale factor *less than* 1 means the drawing is *bigger* or *smaller* than the actual item? _____

18. A scale factor *greater than* 1 means the drawing is *bigger* or *smaller* than the actual item? _____

19. What do you think a scale factor of 1 would mean? _____

Activity 8.2: Money, Money, Money
(Literature)

Objective: Students will convert between various units of currency using passages from three novels involving money. Students will calculate currency values, determine exchange rates, and write formulas to represent the conversion.

Materials & Preparation:

1. Worksheet and pencils

2. Boyce, Frank Cottrrell. *Millions.* New York: HarperCollins, 2004.

3. Clements, Andrew. *Lunch Money.* New York: Simon & Schuster Books for Young Readers, 2005.

4. Rowling, J. K. *Harry Potter and the Sorcerer's Stone.* New York: Scholastic, 1997

5. Access to the media center to find currency exchange rates

Estimated Time: 45-60 minutes

Vocabulary:

currency   exchange rate   convert/conversion   symbol: £

Activity Instructions:

1. Prior to the activity, complete a booktalk about each of the three books to elicit interest in the texts and the topic. Each book references money or "cash" in the currency unique to the location of the text. In *Millions,* the story takes place in England—the book references the Pound Sterling and the Euro. The main character in *Lunch Money* lives in the United States, thus all currency values are in U.S. Dollars. In Harry Potter's world, Galleons, Knuts, and Sickles are used. *Lunch Money* is a great book for a whole class reading.

2. Briefly discuss why it might be helpful to convert the less familiar currencies of British Pounds and Galleons into more familiar U.S. Dollars. How does this information enhance your understanding and appreciation of the story?

3. Provide students with worksheets. Activity can be worked in groups or individually. Answers will vary depending on the current exchange rates. Answers should be rounded to the nearest hundredth, as is customary with U.S. currency rounded to the nearest cent. We provide answers after the worksheet.

Money, Money, Money

In the books *Lunch Money, Millions,* and *Harry Potter and the Sorcerer's Stone,* three units of currency are discussed: U.S. Dollar, British Pound (AKA Pound Sterling), and Harry Potter Galleon.

How do you convert from one unit of money to another?

To convert from one unit of money to another, you must know the *exchange rate.* For example, to convert an amount in U.S. Dollars (US $) to British Pounds (UK £), you need to know how many U.S. Dollars are in a British Pound. Unlike other units of measurement you have converted (inches to centimeters), exchange rates fluctuate, or change. It is important to find the current exchange rate.

U.S. Dollar – British Pound

1. Find the current exchange rate from U.S. Dollars to British Pounds and British Pounds to U.S. Dollars. Round to the nearest hundredth.
    How many U.S. Dollars are in one British Pound? 1 UK £ = _____ US $
    How many British Pounds are in one U.S. Dollar? 1 US $ = _____ UK £

2. You have 10 UK £ and you need to know how much this is in US $. Using the exchange rate you found above for UK £ to US $, circle the operation you will use for your calculation.
    Addition   Subtraction   Multiplication   Division

3. Convert £5 to US $: $_____

4. Convert $5 to UK £: £_____

5. Convert £2.50 to US $: $_____

6. Convert $2.50 to UK £: £ _____

7. Write a formula to convert UK £ to US $. _____

8. Write a formula to convert US $ to UK £. _____

9. How much will Greg earn per day in British pounds? £_____

"If even *half* of those kids had two extra quarters to spend every day, then there had to be at least *four hundred* quarters floating around the school. That was a hundred dollars a day, over *five hundred dollars* each week—money, extra money, just jingling around in pockets and lunch bags!"

– Greg, *Lunch Money,* p. 17

10. How much will Greg earn per week in British pounds? £_____

> "Greg's first business outside his own home was a lemonade stand...His new sign announced: *Greg's ICE COLD Lemonade Still Just 25¢*... Less than an hour later the trouble began. Because there was Maura Shaw, right across the street, setting up her own lemonade sign under a bright beach umbrella with a big sign: *Maura's TASTY LEMONADE only 20¢*."
>
> – *Lunch Money*, p. 46-47

11. How much is Greg's lemonade in UK£? £ _____

12. How much is Maura's lemonade in UK£? £ _____

> "If Anthony was telling this story, he'd start with the money. It always comes down to money, he says, so you might as well start there. He'd probably put, *Once upon a time there were 229,370 little pounds sterling...*"
>
> – Damian, *Millions*, p. 1

13. **Estimate:** How much is £229,370 in U.S. Dollars. $ _____

14. **Calculate:** How much is £229,370 is in U.S. Dollars. $ _____

15. Which has more value: £229,370 or the U.S. Dollar amount you put in question 14? Explain.

_____

_____

> "We have just moved to 7 Cromarty Close...It cost £180,000 but will retain its value well or most likely go up!"
>
> – Damian, *Millions*, p. 16

16. How much would this house cost in U.S. Dollars? _____

17. Damian suggests 7 Cromarty Close may increase in value. If the value of the house increases by 5% how much will it be worth in British Pounds and U.S. Dollars?

£ _____ $ _____

> "So, financially, we had 229,370 pounds sterling. On the morning of December 1 this was worth 323,056 euros."
>
> – Damian, *Millions*, p. 61

18. Based on the information in the passage quoted from page 61, what was the exchange rate from UK£ to Euros on December 1?

    1 UK£ = _____ Euros

19. Suppose on the morning of December 1, £229,370 was equal to $450,000. What is the exchange rate from US $ to Euros?

    1 US $ = _____ Euros

Harry Potter's Money

You've now explored converting between two different monetary systems. But what about converting within one system? Do you know how to do this already? Think about pennies, nickels, dimes, quarters, and dollars. Pretty easy, right? Now try doing it using Harry Potter's Money...

> "Griphook unlocked the door.... Harry gasped. Inside were mounds of gold coins. Columns of silver. Heaps of little bronze Knuts.... Hagrid helped Harry pile some of it into a bag. "The gold ones are Galleons," he explained. "Seventeen silver Sickles to a Galleon and twenty-nine Knuts to a sickle, it's easy enough...."
>
> – *Harry Potter and the Sorcerer's Stone*, p. 75

Answer the questions below and complete Table 8.1.

Ex. How many Sickles in a Galleon? _____17_____

20. How many Knuts in a Sickle? _____

21. How many Knuts in a Galleon? _____

	1 Knut	1 Sickle	1 Galleon
Knut			
Sickle		1	17
Galleon			

Table 8.1 Harry Potter's Money

22 How many Galleons in a Sickle? _____

23. How many Galleons in a Knut? _____

24. How many Sickles in a Knut? _____

After retrieving money from Gringotts, Hagrid and Harry shop at the Apothecary…

"While Hagrid asked the man behind the counter for a supply of some basic potion ingredients for Harry, Harry himself examined silver unicorn horns at twenty-one Galleons each and miniscule, glittery-black beetle eyes (five Knuts a scoop)."

– Harry Potter and the Sorcerer's Stone, p. 81

25. How much would an order of 2 unicorn horns and 6 scoops of beetle eyes cost?

_____ Galleons   _____ Sickles   _____ Knuts

26. If you paid for the above order with 43 Galleons, how much change would you get back?

_____ Galleons   _____ Sickles   _____ Knuts

27. **Estimate:** About how many *Galleons* did Harry pay for the candy? _____ Galleons

"The woman didn't have any Mars Bars. What she did have were Bertie Bott's Every Flavor Beans, Drooble's Best Blowing Gum, Chocolate Frogs, Pumpkin Pastries, Cauldron Cakes, Licorice Wands and a number of other strange things Harry had never seen in his life…he got some of everything and paid the woman eleven silver Sickles and seven bronze Knuts."

– Harry Potter and the Sorcerer's Stone, p. 101

28. **Calculate:** How many *Galleons* did Harry pay for the candy? _____ Galleons

Galleons – U.S. Dollars

On the back of *Fantastic Beasts and Where to Find Them* next to the price of $3.99, it says: "or 14 Sickles 3 Knuts."

29. How many Knuts does the book cost? _____ Knuts

30. How many Galleons does the book cost? _____ Galleons

31. So, $3.99 = _____ Galleons

32. What is the exchange rate from US $ to Galleons?

$$US \$ = \underline{\hspace{2cm}} \text{ Galleons}$$

33. What is the exchange rate from Galleons to US $?

$$1 \text{ Galleon} = \underline{\hspace{2cm}} \text{ US } \$$$

Challenge Questions

"Up on the stage during the awards assembly on the last day of school, Greg Maura, and Mr. Z handed Mrs. Davenport a check for $1,421, a donation to the Ashworth Intermediate School library.... Nine hundred twenty-three dollars and thirty-eight cents of the total donation came directly from the Chunky Comics Group, and Greg Kenton could not believe how good it made him feel to give that money away."

– Lunch Money, p. 222

34. How many Galleons is the check donated to the library? _____ Galleons

35. Put the amount in #33 into: Galleons _____ Sickles _____ Knuts _____

36. How many Galleons did the Chunky Comics Group donate? _____ Galleons

37. Put the amount in #35 into: Galleons _____ Sickles _____ Knuts _____

"Sadly for most of us, the phrase "tons of money" is just a figure of speech. But yesterday thieves made off with literally "tons of money," in used high-denomination sterling notes, earmarked for destruction in the government incinerator in Warrington. The robbery was planned with military precision and a relatively low capital outlay. The final haul could be something in the region of £6,000,000."

– Millions, p. 120.

38. Show the amount stolen in British pounds, U.S. Dollars, and Harry Potter Galleons in Table 8.2.

Pounds	Dollars	Galleons
£6,000,000		

Table 8.2 Pounds Dollars Galleons

39. A millionaire is "a person whose wealth is estimated at a million or more." How many U.S. Dollars do you need to be a millionaire in the United Kingdom? In the Wizardly World of Harry Potter?

United Kingdom $ _____   Wizardly World $ _____

Definition for "millionaire" from <www.Merriam-Webster.com>.

Question 1: Use an online currency converter to find current exchange rates.

Example: 1 UK £ = ___1.98___ US $

1 US $ = ___.51___ UK £

Questions 2 - 6: Students should discover that they will use *multiplication* to convert from £ to $, by multiplying £10 by the exchange rate. Students will then perform conversions from £ to $ and vice versa using whole numbers and decimals. Answers will vary based on the exchange rates found in Question 1.

Questions 7 & 8: A formula to represent the conversion should look similar to the one below. The coefficient used will vary based on the exchange rates found in Question 1.

£ to $ = $x \cdot 1.98$ or $1.98x$

$ to £ = $x \cdot .51$ or $.51x$

Questions 9 & 10: Students should multiply 100 by the US $ to UK£ exchange rate to find the daily earnings, and multiply 500 by the US $ to UK£ exchange rate to find the weekly earnings.

Questions 11 & 12: Students should correctly represent 25¢ and 20¢ as $0.25 and $0.20, respectively, prior to multiplying by the US $ to UK£ exchange rate.

Questions 13 & 14: Everyday involvement with money often requires people to make estimations (such as tip amounts and sale prices). As such, ask students to estimate how much the money is in U.S. dollars prior to making the actual calculation.

Question 15 Assesses the student's understanding of the concept "value" and provides an opportunity to communicate mathematically. Despite there being more pounds than dollars quantitatively, students should understand they both represent the same value.

Questions 16 & 17: Students multiply 180,000 by the UK£ to US $ exchange rate to find the value of the home in U.S. Dollars. Students then determine the increased value of the home of £189,000 prior to converting to U.S. Dollars. Common error: Student may calculate the increase by multiplying 180,000 by 5% yielding $9000, and not solve any further. Problem requires students to *add* the increase to the original value to obtain £189,000.

Questions 18 & 19: Students are provided two equivalent units of currency and are asked to calculate the exchange rate. 323,056/229,370 = ~1.41 Similarly, 450,000/229,370 =~1.96 This is a good opportunity to discuss approximations and how a small rounding up in the hundredths place affects larger numbers like those used in the questions. For example, multiplying 1.41 by 229,370 = 323,411, a measurable difference of 335.70 Euros from the original 323,056. "If you were cashing in your pounds for Euros, would you want them to use the rounded exchange rate?" "What if you owned the bank?" "What if they rounded down, instead of up?

Questions 20 - 23: The story tells us there are 29 Knuts in a Sickle, and 17 Sickles in a Galleon. So, there must be 29*17 = 493 Knuts in a Galleon. Since there are 29 Knuts in a Sickle, 1 Knut is 1/29 of a Sickle or ~.034. Likewise, 1 Knut is 1/493 of a Galleon or ~.002. Lastly, a Sickle is 1/17 of a Galleon, or ~.059. If students are having difficulty, have them create a similar chart to the one in

Table 8.3 with dollars, quarters, dimes, nickels, and pennies and then attempt to complete with the less familiar and non-decimalized Knuts, Sickles, and Galleons.

	1 Knut	1 Sickle	1 Galleon
Knut	1	29	493
Sickle	~.034	1	17
Galleon	~.002	~.059	1

Table 8.3 Harry Potter Money Answer

Questions 24 & 25:

(2 * 21 Galleons) + (6 * 5 Knuts) = 42 Galleons 30 Knuts or 42 Galleons 1 Sickle 1 Knut

43 Galleons – 42 Galleons 1 Sickle 1 Knut = 15 Sickles 28 Knuts

Questions 26 & 27: Since there are 17 Sickles in a Galleon, and Harry paid at least 11 Sickles, students should estimate a number greater than 1/2 Galleon but less than 1 Galleon.

11 Sickles + 7 Knuts = (.059 * 11) + (.002 * 7) = .663 Galleons

Question 28: 14 Sickles 3 Knuts = (14 * 29) + 3 = 409 Knuts

Questions 29 -31: Since there are 493 Knuts in a Galleon, the book is 409/493 Galleons or ~.83 Galleons. So, $3.99 = .83 Galleons

Question 32: $3.99 = .83 Galleons, dividing each side by 3.99 yields 1 US $ = .21 Galleons

Question 33: $3.99 = .83 Galleons, dividing each side by .83 yields 1 Galleons = $4.81

Questions 34 & 35: $1,421 = 1421 *.21 = 298.41 Galleons .41 Galleons = ~202 Knuts = 6 Sickles 28 Knuts. So, the check is equal to ~298 Galleons 6 Sickles 28 Knuts.

Questions 36 & 37: $923.38= 923.48 * .21 = 193.93 Galleons .93 Galleons = ~ 458 Knuts = 15 Sickles 23 Knuts. So, the check is equal to ~193 Galleons 15 Sickles 23 Knuts.

Question 38: This question requires two steps to complete the conversion, from Pounds to Dollars and from Dollars to Galleons. Answer may vary based on the UK£ to US $ exchange rate found in question 1.

Ex. £6,000,000 = 6,000,000 * 1.98 = $11,880,000

$11,880,000 = 11,880,000 * .21 = 2,494,800 Galleons

Question 39: The question is asking, "how many U.S. Dollars do you need to get 1 million UK£ and 1 million Galleons…" Answer may vary based on the UK£ to US $ exchange rate in question 1.

Ex. £ 1,000,000 = 1,000,000 * .51 = $510,000

Activity 8.3: Sizing Up Sports
(Environmental Print)

Objective: Students will determine the area and perimeter of various sports fields and make comparisons with the calculations.

Materials & Preparation:
Worksheet

Estimated Time:
45-60 minutes

Activity Instructions:

1. Use the relevant data from sports to help students understand the difference between perimeter and area and how to calculate each. Question students prior to activity to ensure correct understanding. Ex. *Would the person who lines the field need to know the perimeter or area of the field to calculate how much paint s/ he needs? What about the person who mows the grass? Perimeter determines how much border you might need in a room; area determines how much carpet you would need to cover the floor.*

2. Let students work through the worksheet. Answers to follow.

Sizing Up Sports

1 mile = 5,280 feet   1 meter = 3.28 feet

1. Fill in Table 8.4 with the perimeter and area of the various sports playing fields.

	Length	Width	Perimeter	Area
NFL Football Field	120 yards	53 1/3 yards		
NBA Basketball Court	94 feet	50 feet		
Soccer Field	100 yards	60 yards		
Lacrosse Field	110 yards	60 yards		
Rugby Field	144 meters	70 meters		

Table 8.4 Sports Field Measurements

2. As a penalty, the coach says you must run around the perimeter of one of the playing fields in the table. Rank the five playing fields from longest distance to shortest distance:

   1.
   2.
   3.
   4.
   5.

3. Coach offers two choices: once around the $^1/4$-mile track *or* twice the length of the lacrosse field. Which is farther? _____

4. Players typically run mostly in the area of the playing field. Rank the 5 playing fields from most area to least area.

   1.
   2.
   3.
   4.
   5.

SOMETHING TO THINK ABOUT:
Are your lists in Questions 2 & 4 the same?

5. The dimensions of the opening of a soccer, field hockey, and lacrosse goal are shown in Table 8.6.

In which sport does the goalie cover the most area? _____

In which sport does a player have the smallest area to score a goal?

_____

Sport	Goal Opening Area
Lacrosse	36 sq. ft.
Field Hockey	84 sq. ft.
Soccer	192 sq. ft.

Table 8.6 Goal Measurement Answers

6. Distance between bases on a Major League Baseball (MLB) baseball field is 90 feet. Which player has the farthest distance to run in their warm-up:
   a. Basketball: runs the length of the court 5 times
   b. Football: runs the perimeter of the field
   c. Rugby: runs the width of the field twice
   d. Baseball: 2 loops through the bases

7. Do an Internet search with the following criteria in the search window:

+MLB +stadium +dimensions

(If provided, click: "Search Images.") Locate images of the park layouts for: Fenway Park, Coors Field, Minute Maid Park, and Yankee Stadium. Look closely at the outfield design of those parks specifically. Examine the general field shape, outfield dimensions, and overall configuration. Write a few sentences about which park you think it would be easier to hit a home run in and why.

Here are the four stadiums ranked from most likely to score home runs to least likely: Coors Stadium, Yankee Stadium, Minute Maid Park, and Fenway Park. Compare your analysis to ESPN! <www.espn.go.com>

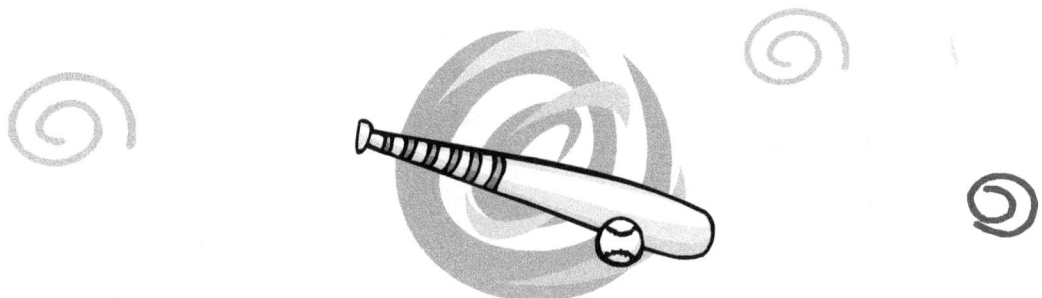

	Length	Width	Perimeter	Perimeter in sq ft	Area	Area in sq ft
NFL Football Field	120 yards	53 1/3 yards	346 2/3 yards	1040	6400 sq. yards	57600
NBA Basketball Court	94 feet	50 feet	288 feet	228	4700 sq. feet	4700
Soccer Field	100 yards	60 yards	320 yards	960	6000 sq. yards	54000
Lacrosse Field	110 yards	60 yards	340 yards	1020	6600 sq. yards	59400
Rugby Field	144 meters	70 meters	428 meter	1403	10080 sq. meters	~10,8444

Table 8.5 Sports Field Measurement Answers

Rankings by Perimeter
1. Rugby
2. Football
3. Lacrosse
4. Soccer
5. Basketball

Rankings by Area
1. Rugby
2. Lacrosse
3. Football
4. Soccer
5. Basketball

Notice the two lists are different. Despite the football field having a greater perimeter distance, the lacrosse field has a larger area.

Question 3: The track run is farther. A quarter of a mile is 1,320 feet. Twice the lacrosse field is only 660 feet.

Question 5: The soccer goalie must cover the most area, while the lacrosse player has the smallest goal area in which to score.

Sport	Goal Opening Area
Lacrosse	36 sq. ft.
Field Hockey	84 sq. ft.
Soccer	192 sq. ft.

Table 8.6 Goal Measurement Answers

Question 6: The longest warm-up is running the perimeter of the football field because: a: 94*5 = 470 feet, b: 1040 feet, c: 459.2 feet, and d. 90*4=360 * 2 = 720 feet.

Question 7: This final question provides an opportunity for students to think about measurement in relation to other factors involved. There is no correct answer, so students will simply make conjectures about the measurements.

Possible Variables:
> *Right-handed or left-handed batter*
> *Altitude of the park*
> *Stadium Construction affecting how air is channeled through the park*
> *   and thus the movement of the ball*
> *Placement of the outfield wall*
> *Wind speed and direction*
> *Temperature and humidity*
> *Pitch thrown*

Based on ESPN park factors, here are the four stadiums ranked from most likely to score home runs to least likely: 1. Coors; 2. Yankee Stadium; 3. Minute Maid; 4. Fenway Park

Chapter 9

Data Analysis and Probability

Activity 9.1: Probability, Possibility, and Serendipity (Informational Text)

Objective: Students will complete an anticipation guide prior to reading real-world statistical information. The guide will be used to compare students' perceptions within the class and as a source of comparison with the actual data. Students will read other types of text to gain a wider perspective about the role of probability in their world.

Materials & Preparation:

1. Paper and 9 sticky notes, one set for each group of 4 students

2. Ball, Johnny. *Go Figure! A Totally Cool Book about Numbers*. New York: DK Publishing, 2005, p. 77.

3. Burger, Edward B., and Michael Starbird. *Coincidences, Chaos, and All That Math Jazz: Making Light of Weighty Ideas*. New York: W.W. Norton & Company, 2005, pp. 56-58.

Activity 9.1: Probability, Possibility, and Serendipity continued

4. Rulers

5. Holland, Bart K. *What Are the Chances?: Voodoo Deaths, Office Gossip, and Other Adventures in Probability.* Baltimore, MD: The Johns Hopkins University Press, 2002, p. 72.

6. Fadiman, Clifton. *The Mathematical Magpie.* New York: Copernicus. pp. 15-19: Coates, Robert M., "The Law."

Estimated Time: 1-2 class periods

Activity Instructions:

This is a discussion activity providing suggested readings from informational texts about probability and chance. Topics include causes of death, commercial airline safety, psychic powers, and the law of averages. The collection provides a wider perspective of what we think is likely and unlikely, and why. Furthermore, it allows for a dialogue about how statistical and non-statistical information shapes public perception. A pre-reading activity known as an anticipation guide is provided for the first reading to stimulate prior knowledge and get students thinking about important ideas prior to reading. Similar guides can be created for the other readings.

RISKY BUSINESS

"Some people are terrified of lightning but happy to smoke. If they understood probability, they might think differently."

– Go Figure! p. 77

In a section about chance, *Go Figure!* contains interesting statistical information about the probability of dying from certain causes. The graphic lists nine causes of death with a "chance of dying in a year." (Struck by lightning is near the bottom at 1 in 10 million while smoking tops the list at 1 in 200.)

Rank the Causes of Death from Most Likely to Least Likely

1.

2.

3.

4.

5.

6.

7.

8.

9.

Activity 9.1: Probability, Possibility, and Serendipity continued

Anticipation Guide Activity: In groups of 3-4 students, provide the listed nine causes of death (one cause per sticky note) and a sheet similar to the one shown. Have students rank the causes of death from most likely to least likely. Each group should share their group's list with the class. Conduct a class discussion, analyzing the data to find similarities and differences. *What information did you use to determine the placement of sticky notes? Were you influenced by any personal experiences or group member?* Use the group data to create one overall class list.

Read the text in *Go Figure!* Compare the text with the class list. *How similar was our list to the actual results? What factors could affect the probabilities of the listed causes of death? If you lived in Africa, do you think the likelihood of some of the causes of death might increase? Which ones might decrease? What about age—do you think the chances listed in the book would be the same for a 15-year-old and a 50-year-old? What about if you are male or female? Notice the probabilities are listed as "chance of dying in a year"; how does that differ from lifetime odds?*

Using the "chance of dying in a year" statistical information, launch a discussion on the range of 0-1 in probability with 1 indicating certainty and 0 meaning impossibility. *The probability of 1 in 200 can also be written as 1/200 or .005, which is between 0 and 1. 1 in 10 million can be written 1/10 million or .0000001. Which value is closer to 0, .005 or .0000001? Which is closer to 1? What do you think a probability of "0" means? What about a probability of "1"? What about .50? (Provide or elicit examples of each scenario.)*

What is the leading cause of fatalities for teens? According to the National Safety Council (NSC), "Traffic crashes account for 44% of teen deaths in the U.S." <www.nsc.org/issues/teendriving/>

AIR SAFETY

"Over the past decade or so, on average there have been approximately 183 deaths per year in commercial airline accidents, which is about one death every two days or one death every 3.4 billion passenger-miles.... Let's try to put the rate of one death for every 3.4 billion passenger-mile in perspective. Suppose a particular individual flew 1,000 miles each day. On average, it would take that person 3.4 million days of flying—that is, 3.4 billion divided by 1,000—before he or she was killed in an airline accident. That many days comes to roughly 10,000 years."

– *Coincidences, Chaos, and All That Math Jazz, p. 56-58*

Activity 9.1: Probability, Possibility, and Serendipity continued

Interestingly, the text says money spent to increase airline safety could cause airline ticket prices to go up resulting in air passengers resorting to driving instead. While airline deaths would decrease, deaths *overall* would increase due to the more dangerous choice of car travel. This presents an opportunity to explain how certain events affect the probability of other events positively and negatively. *What do you think might happen if airlines are made less safe? Despite the data, why do some people feel like flying is unsafe and drive rather than fly? What factors might affect your perception of air travel and its overall safety? Do you think, if provided the statistical information, people who think air travel is dangerous might change their mind?*

Is it really more dangerous on the way to the airport than the flight itself? YES.
"The National Safety Council (NSC) lists lifetime odds of dying in a motor vehicle accident at 1 in 84, while air and space travel deaths odds are 1 in 5,051." (This includes non-commercial air travel, so most likely commercial travel deaths would be even lower.) <www.nsc.org/lrs/statinfo/odds.htm>

What is the most dangerous holiday? "The combination of travel, alcohol and fireworks has made July the nation's deadliest month and the 4th of July our most dangerous holiday." <www.nsc.org/news/julyholidayrelease.htm>

PSYCHIC POWERS

"On any given night in a large city, people have millions of dreams. Lots of dreams are nonsense, but people do dream about known individuals and possible events. It should hardly be surprising that some matches with reality do occur, given a staggering number of both dreams and potentially matching events from which to choose…. However, it is difficult to assess the rate at which matches with reality occur, because the reports that reach your ears tell only of dreams that came true, while matches are only a part of the story. Such dreams tend to send a shiver down the spine because they are often regarded as a demonstration of 'psychic powers.'"

– *What Are the Chances?* p. 72

Ask students for examples from their own personal experiences with coincidences. Is probability involved? For example, if you compare many details about two people (birthdates, family names, occupations, and so on) isn't there some likelihood there will be things in common? What about the famous comparisons between Abraham Lincoln and John F. Kennedy? For all the coincidences, there are also many things not similar. Discuss the role of probability in psychic ability. If a psychic talks about someone in your family, why do you think they use the name "John" or "Michael" instead of a less common name? For example, how many of you have someone in your family named "John?"

Activity 9.1: Probability, Possibility, and Serendipity continued

Another section titled "Miracles" on pages 90-91 of *What Are the Chances?* provides the probability of a series of events, leaving the reader to decide if the coincidence were examples of "divine providence at work."

Literature Extension: "The Law," a short story in the book *The Mathematical Magpie*, describes a world in which there is no law of averages: a notion that the past does not predict the probability of future occurrences in the long term. In the story, the end result is catastrophic—affecting everything from traffic patterns and store inventories to theater patronage, and lunchroom item availability. *Have you heard of the expression, "Law of Averages?" What do you think it means?* Read the passage and ask again. *Many say it is the way things balance out in the world in which we live, or as Coates says, "on the basis of past experience it had always been possible to foretell" the future. Does the probability of one event really affect another? (i.e., are life events independent or dependent?) If one person orders pastrami does this really increase or decrease the likelihood of someone else* not *ordering pastrami? Is there probability involved? Discuss how companies use statistical information to make predictions about the future in many ways: how many seats to put in a theater, where to build new highways, how much bread to order at the local store, how much oil to import, and so on...isn't this all based on the likelihood or probability of what people will do, eat, use?*

One of the primary concerns with storm predications is the speculation how people will react—everyone might buy water, or withdraw $100 in cash from the ATM, thus violating the "law of averages."

Note: "The Law" is a great whole class reading.

Activity 9.2: The Missing Merrill
(Literature)

Objective: Students will use real world data to create a scatter plot, estimate a line-of-best-fit, and find correlations to solve a mystery.

Materials & Preparation:

1. Pencils
2. Brown, Jeremy. *Crime Files: Four Minute Forensic Mysteries: Body of Evidence.* New York: Scholastic, Inc., 2006. For this activity students will read the short story "The Missing Merrill," pp.156-158, so you will need multiple copies.
3. Copies of data sheet
4. Blank scatter plot for students to plot data
5. Copies of "evidence" for each group: photo of a humerus bone
6. Measuring tapes
7. Linguini , uncooked

Estimated Time: 45-60 minutes

Activity Instructions:

1. Write instructions for the reading on a transparency or on the board: *Ask students to circle unknown words as they read, and underline words that they think are possible clues or helpful information.*
2. Read "The Missing Merrill" aloud to the class.
3. Question students: "What words did we circle?" *Help students define unknown words by eliciting information from the class.* "What words did we underline?" *Students should offer the x-ray, Mr. Merrill's height, and the estimation of the wife's height—3/4 of Mr. Merrill's height.* "Does anyone have an idea how Detective Burton knew this was not the body of Mrs. Merrill? Do you think the length of the humerus had some indication of her height?"
4. Once students surmise that the length of the humerus must have something to do with height, discuss how it can be proven using a scatter plot.
5. Divide students into groups: 4+ students/group.
6. Advise students to use the instructions to guide measurements.
7. Students plot their data from the data sheet onto the provided graph.
8. Ask students to interpret their scatter plot to see if there is a positive, negative, or no correlation between their two variables. How do you know?
9. Ask students to use the linguini to estimate a line-of-best-fit.
10. Students should then see that there is a correlation between the height of a person and their humerus length. Then ask students to locate the length of the humerus in the x-ray on their line-of-best-fit. *What is the approximate height of the body? How does this compare with the height of Mrs. Merrill? Is the body the body of Mrs. Merrill?* Students should find the height of the body would be much taller than the height of Mrs. Merrill.

Data Sheet

1. RECORD each group member's height in inches in the height column.
   * 1 foot = 12 inches

2. MEASURE & RECORD the humerus of group members.

Bend arm at 90° angle.

Start tape at highest rounded part of humerus. Locate one of the two ends of the humerus on either side of elbow. Record measurement in the length column.

3. Use X-ray to MEASURE & RECORD arm length of body.

4. Plot each member's height and bone length on graph. Since our data is incomplete for the body, do not plot the body's information.

Group Member Name	Height (in inches)	Length of humerus (in inches)
1		
2		
3		
4		
5		
6		
BODY	Information not available	

Table 9.1 Member Measurements

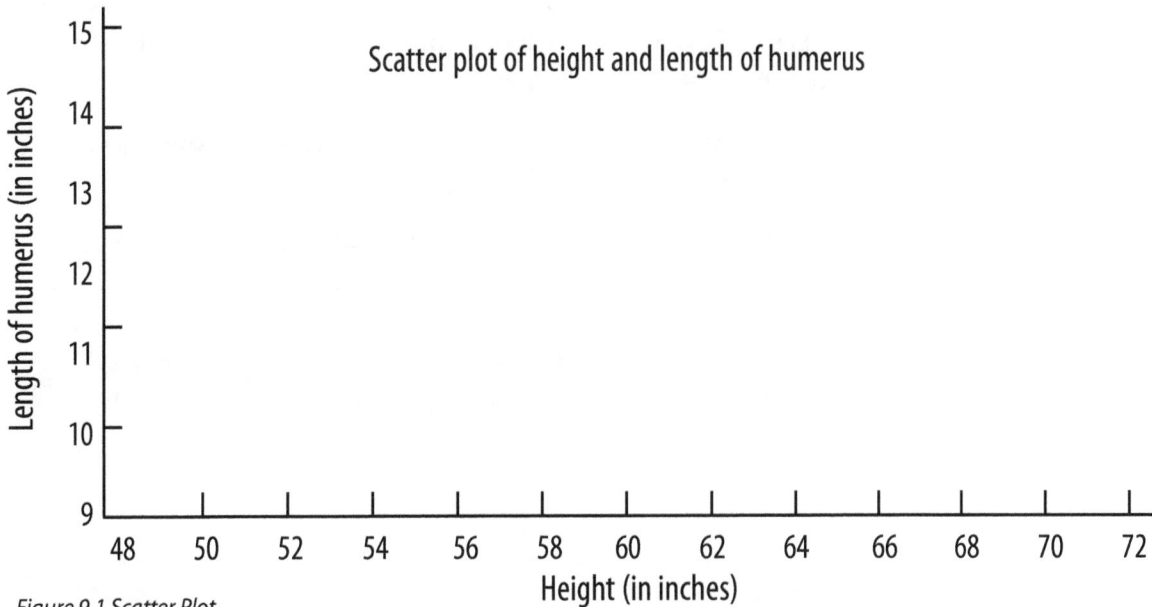

Figure 9.1 Scatter Plot

Activity 93: Is There ESP?
(Literature)

Objective: Students will recreate one of the "Paranormal Pursuits" projects in Mind Games and document data results. Students will collect, organize, and analyze data, and interpret the results by determining mean, median, mode, constructing a line plot and a graph, and comparing their results with the experiments completed in the book.

Materials & Preparation:

1. Deck of 25 Zener ESP cards (5 of each symbol: star, plus, wavy lines, square, circle). These can be pre-made using our template or students can create their own.

2. ESP experiment packet/pencils

3. Grunwell, Jeanne Marie. *Mind Games.* Houghton Mifflin Company: Boston, 2003.

Estimated Time: 2-3 day project

Activity Instructions:

1. Read pages 23-30. This section describes the science fair project and ESP-related vocabulary.

2. Read pages 55-76. This section describes the experiment, the results, and the analysis.

3. Provide each student with the ESP packet.

4. Students create a deck of Zener cards and conduct their own ESP experiments with 5 subjects and complete the packet.

   - Collect data: Students should follow the instructions for conducting the Zener test using 5 subjects.

   - Organize data: Students should determine the number correct for each subject, the percent correct for each subject, and the mean, median, and mode for the total group. The minimum number correct is 0, maximum is 25 for a range of 0-25. The sample size is 5, since 5 subjects were tested. The line plot should be neat, titled appropriately, and accurately represent the data collected. The graph should also meet these criteria, but should also include labels on the axes and demonstrate an understanding of appropriate use of scale for the axes. The last two questions provide students with an opportunity to create a circle graph, thus creating a snapshot of their results.

- Analyze data: In answering questions 11 and 12, an analysis of their data and the data in *Mind Games* should be complemented by a greater discussion about sampling and trials. Students should realize the sampling used in *Mind Games* was not random since only those who scored well in the pre-test were used in the experiment. Provide examples of random and non-random sampling, and the bias and skewed results that would be inherent in using non-random sampling. It is important to discuss the importance of why more than 20% correct is significant. In the experiments by Zener in the 1930s, a score greater than 20% (or significantly lower than 20%, as in the case of 0%) was often considered a sign of something more than just chance. Ideally, this discussion should lead to a discussion of trials—the more trials performed, the more data is available, and the more convincing the results. In *Mind Games*, two trials are performed with differing outcomes for the twin sisters, providing some evidence of the need for multiple trials.

Is There ESP?

Role: Parapsychologist.

Task: Conduct an ESP Zener card test with 5 people (subjects) and construct a graph representing the number of corrects answers provided by the subjects.

Follow these steps to complete the ESP test:

1. Shuffle the cards.
2. Sit in a room with the subject, but make sure they cannot see the cards.
3. Take a card; concentrate on the symbol on the card. Do not talk.
4. The subject guesses the symbol on the card.
5. Do not indicate if the subject's response was correct or not.
6. Record the response on the sheet below using "**x**" for incorrect and "✓" for correct.
7. Repeat with all 25 cards.

	subject # 1	subject # 2	subject # 3	subject # 4	subject # 5
1					
2					
3					
4					
5					
6					
7					
8					
9					
10					
11					
12					
13					
14					
15					
16					
17					
18					
19					
20					
21					
22					
23					
24					
25					

Table 9.2 ESP Zener Card Test

8. Using your collected data, complete Table 9.3.

subject	# of correct responses	# correct / # guessed	percent correct?
#1		_____ / 25	_____ %
#2		_____ / 25	_____ %
#3		_____ / 25	_____ %
#4		_____ / 25	_____ %
#5		_____ / 25	_____ %

Table 9.3 ESP Zener Card Test Data

9. Is this categorical or numeric data? _____

10. Determine the mean, median, and mode **number of correct responses**.

   Mean_____   **Median** _____   **Mode**_____

11. What is the *minimum* number of responses a subject could answer correctly? _____

12. What is the *maximum* number of responses a subject could answer correctly? _____

13. What is the sample size in your experiment? _____

14. In a graph showing the number of correct answers for each subject, what is the range of data? _____

15. Construct a line plot showing the number of correct answers for each subject.

16. Construct a graph of your choice to best represent the information in the line plot.

17. On page 55, Ji says, "The first experiment our group did was a pretest to increase our chances of finding someone with ESP. We got as many people as we could to do the Zener ESP card test. We decided to do more testing on only the subjects who scored the best." Does their experiment use random sampling? Why or why not?

18. On pages 59-60, data and comments for Benjamin's ESP test are shown. He writes, "May I also point out that my test results here are noteworthy for being significantly *lower* than those expected by chance (which would be 5 correct, or 20%)... I would have guessed the same symbol 25 times and been assured of attaining a decent score of 20%." What do you think he meant?

19. On page 62, Brandon guesses all the same symbol, proving what Benjamin stated earlier. How many of *your* experiments scored:

More than 20% correct _____   **Less than 20% correct** _____

20. Complete the circle graph with your data from question #13.

Figure 9.2 Circle

21. Using your data in question #14, is there ESP?

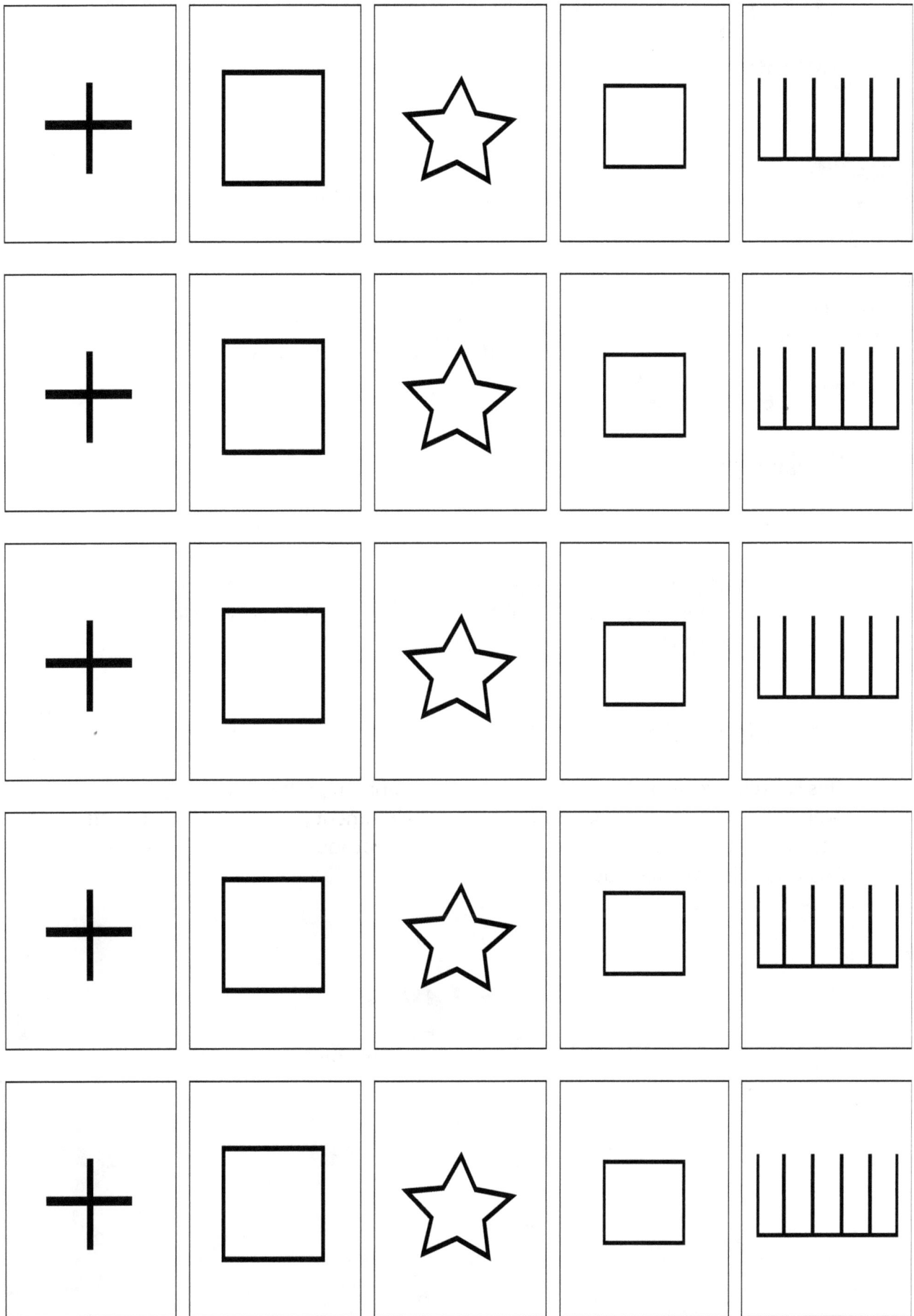

Figure 9.3 ESP Cards

Activity 94: Lottery Lingo
(Environmental)

Objective: Students will apply probability vocabulary using information from lottery tickets.

Materials & Preparation:

1. Sample bubble-in lottery forms, scratch-off tickets
2. Attached worksheet

Estimated Time: 45-60 minutes

Vocabulary:

outcomes	odds	dependent
event	combinations	independent
experiment	equally likely	complementary
impossible, certainty	probability	mutually exclusive
sample space	simple event	

Activity Instructions:

This is a reinforcing activity to be used during a unit on probability to highlight probability and statistical vocabulary. Using environment print such as scratch-off lottery tickets and game slips, students apply the vocabulary in a familiar context. Answers follow the handout.

Lottery Lingo

Think of the last time you watched as a lottery drawing of ping-pong balls revealed the night's winning lottery numbers on live television. Using the word bank below, fill in the appropriate terms:

outcomes   event   experiment   impossible
sample space   dependent   independent

1. Drawing three numbers from a set of balls numbered 1-9. _____

2. Three lottery numbers are drawn and the results are: 9, 1, 7. _____

3. The machine contains balls numbered 1-56. A ball is drawn and not replaced. Drawing a ball numbered 20 on the second draw is _____ of the first draw.

4. Drawing a ball numbered 52 from a set of balls numbered 1 to 39. _____

5. "The odds of matching all 5 numbers are: 1 in 575,757." 575,757 is the total number of possible _____.

6. The set of all possible outcomes for rolling a pair of dice. _____

7. The machine contains balls numbered 1-46. 5 balls are drawn and then replaced. A power ball is then drawn. Drawing a ball numbered 20 on the power ball is _____ of the first five draws.

Mega Millions	Fantasy 5
Select five numbers from 1 to 56	Select 5 numbers from 1 to 39

Table 9.4 Mega Millions and Fantasy 5

8. Compare the range of numbers to select from in Mega Millions to Fantasy 5. Which game do you think has better odds of matching all 5 numbers? _____ Why?

9. Once a ball is drawn from the ball set it is not replaced. If they replace the ball each time it is drawn before drawing the next number, how would this affect the odds of winning?
   a. odds of winning would increase

b. no change in odds of winning

c. odds of winning would decrease

Big Bucks	Money Bags
Overall odds 1:3.72	Overall odds 1:4.50
Cost per ticket: $3	Cost per ticket: $1

Table 9.5 Big Bucks and Money Bags

10. Look at Table 9.5. One option has better odds but costs more. The other costs less but has worse odds. Which is the better deal? If you purchase 3 MONEY BAGS, spending the same as one BIG BUCKS ticket, what happens to the odds of winning MONEY BAGS?

    a. odds of winning would increase

    b. no change in odds of winning

    c. odds of winning would decrease

11. Cash 3 allows you to select a 3-digit number from 000-999 and can be played several different ways. You selected the 3-digit number 123. List all the possible *winning* combinations for each of the ways to play Cash 3 in Table 9.6.

Game play	List all the combinations of outcomes that would result in a win
Straight—match all 3 numbers in exact order	
Box—match all 3 numbers in any order	
Front Pair—match only the first two numbers	
Back Pair—match only the last two numbers	

Table 9.6 Big Bucks and Money Bags

12. During the news the Cash 3 numbers are announced, 7 7 7. Surprised, the anchor person says, "What are the chances!" After drawing the first 7, the odds for drawing a second 7:
    a. increased
    b. remained the same
    c. decreased

The probability of a simple event is = number of ways and event can occur divided by number of possible outcomes

13. In a machine containing nine balls numbered 1-9, what is the probability of drawing a 5?

14. In a machine containing nine balls numbered 1-9, what is the probability of drawing an odd number?

15. In a machine containing nine balls numbered 1-9, what is the probability of drawing a 0?

16. In a machine containing nine balls all numbered 6, what is the probability of drawing a 6?

17. TRUE or FALSE: In a machine containing nine balls numbered 1-9, each of the balls has an equally likely chance of being drawn. _____

18. TRUE or FALSE: In a machine containing nine balls numbered 1-9, the chance of drawing an odd-numbered ball and the chance of drawing an even-numbered ball are equally likely. _____

19. TRUE or FALSE: In the lottery, winning and losing are mutually exclusive.

20. TRUE or FALSE: In the lottery, winning and losing are complementary

Question 1: Drawing three numbers from a set of balls numbered 1-9. **experiment**

Question 2: Three lottery numbers are drawn and the results are: 9, 1, 7. **Event**

Question 3: The machine contains balls numbered 1-56. A ball is drawn and not replaced. Drawing ball number 20 on the second draw is **dependent** on the first draw.

Question 4: Drawing a ball numbered 52 from a set of balls numbered 1 to 39. **Impossible**

Question 5: 575,757 is the total number of possible **outcomes**.

Question 6: The set of all possible outcomes for rolling a pair of dice. **sample space**

Question 7: The machine contains balls numbered 1-46. 5 balls are drawn and then replaced. A power ball is then drawn. Drawing ball number 20 on the power ball is **independent** of the first five draws.

Question 8: The MEGA MILLIONS has better odds of winning since the set of possible numbers to select is smaller.

Question 9: Replacing the ball between drawings would result in a decrease in odds of winning.

Question 10: MONEY BAGS is the better deal. If you purchase 3 tickets you only need to win on one ticket to win. This is an OR situation, therefore you would add the probabilities of each ticket to get the overall odds of winning 1 / 4.5 + 1 / 4.5 + 1 / 4.5 = 2/3. 2:3 (.666) is much better odds than 1:3.72 (.269).

Question 11: See Table 9.7 for answer.

Game play	List all the combinations of outcomes that would result in a win
Straight—match all 3 numbers in exact order	1 2 3
Box—match all 3 numbers in any order	1 2 3 1 3 2 2 3 1 2 1 3 3 2 1 3 1 2
Front Pair—match only the first two numbers	1 2 0 1 2 1 1 2 2 1 2 3 1 2 4 1 2 5 1 2 6 1 2 7 1 2 8 1 2 9
Back Pair—match only the last two numbers	0 2 3 1 2 3 2 2 3 3 2 3 4 2 3 5 2 3 6 2 3 7 2 3 8 2 3 9 2 3

Table 9.7 Lottery Game Play Answer

Question 12: b. On the first drawing, the probability of drawing a 7 was 1:9. The probability of drawing a 7 on the second draw was also 1:9. Therefore, the odds of drawing a 7 on the second ball remained the same.

Question 13: Probability of drawing a 5: 1/9 or 1:9

Question 14: Probability of drawing an odd number: 5/9 or 5:9

Question 15: Probability of drawing a 0: 0/9 or 0

Question 16: Probability of drawing a 6: 9/9 or 1

Question 17: TRUE.

Question 18: FALSE. The odds of drawing an odd number are: 5:9, while the odds of drawing an even number are 4:9.

Question 19: TRUE. Winning or losing are mutually exclusive since you either can win or lose, but you can't get both.

Question 20: TRUE. Winning and losing are complementary events since the odds of winning plus the odds of losing would equal 1.

Works Cited

Ball, Johnny. *Go Figure! A Totally Cool Book about Numbers*. New York: DK Publishing, 2005.

Balliett, Blue. *Chasing Vermeer*. NY: Scholastic, 2004.

—. *The Wright 3*. New York: Scholastic Press, 2006.

Blatner, David. *The Joy of Pi*. New York: Walker and Company, 1997.

Boyce, Frank Cottrell. *Millions*. New York: HarperCollins, 2004.

Boyle, David, and Anita Roddick. *Numbers*. West Sussex, UK: Anita Roddick Books, 2004.

Brown, Jeremy. *Crime Files: Four Minute Forensic Mysteries: Shadow of Doubt*. New York: Scholastic, 2006.

Burger, Edward B., and Michael Starbird. *Coincidences, Chaos, and All That Math Jazz: Making Light of Weighty Ideas*. New York: W.W. Norton & Company, 2005.

Clements, Andrew. *Lunch Money*. New York: Simon & Schuster Books for Young Readers, 2005.

Collins, Suzanne. *Gregor and the Code of Claw*. New York: Scholastic, 2007.

Eastaway, Rob, and Jeremy Wyndham. *Why Do Buses Come in Threes? The Hidden Mathematics of Everyday Life*. New York: John Wiley & Sons, Inc., 1998.

Enzensberger, Hans Mangus. *The Number Devil: A Mathematical Adventure*. Trans. Michael Henry Heim. New York: Henry Holt and Company, 2000.

Evans, Mary Anna. *Artifacts*. Scottsdale, AZ: Poisoned Pen Press, 2003.

—. *Effigies*. Arizona: Poisoned Pen Press, 2007.

—. *Relics*. Arizona: Poisoned Pen Press, 2005.

Fadiman, Clifton. *The Mathematical Magpie*. New York: Copernicus, 1962.

Fantastic Feats and Failures. Tonawanda, NY: Kids Can Press, 2004.

Green, John. *An Abundance of Katherines*. New York: Dutton Books, 2006.

Grunwell, Jeanne Marie. *Mind Games*. Boston: Houghton Mifflin, 2003.

Harris, Nicholas, and Sebastian Quigley. *How Big Are They?* Baltimore, MD: Flying Frog Publishing/Allied Publishing, 2004.

Holland, Bart K. *What Are the Chances?: Voodoo Deaths, Office Gossip, and Other Adventures in Probability*. Baltimore, MD: The Johns Hopkins University Press, 2002.

Holtz, Andrew. *The Facts Behind the Addictive Medical Drama: The Medical Science of House, M.D.* New York: Penguin, 2006.

Isdell, Wendy. *A Gebra Named Al*. Minneapolis, MN: Free Spirit Publishing Inc., 1993.

Janeczko, Paul B. *Top Secret: A Handbook of Codes, Ciphers, and Secret Writing*. Cambridge, MA: Candlewick Press, 2004

Jinks, Catherine. *Evil Genius*. New York: Harcourt, 2007.

Juster, Norton. *The Phantom Tollbooth*. New York: Dell Yearling, 1961.

Klages, Ellen. *The Green Glass Sea*. New York: Viking, 2006.

Langford, David. *Different Kinds of Darkness*. Rockville, MD: Cosmos Books, an Imprint of Wildside Press, 2004.

Lewis, Michael. *Moneyball: The Art of Winning an Unfair Game*. New York: W.W. Norton & Company, 2004.

Luper, Eric. *Big Slick: High Stakes and Dirty Laundry*. New York: Farrar, Strauss and Giroux, 2007.

Martinez, Joseph G.R., and Nancy C. Martinez. *Reading and Writing to Learn Mathematics: A Guide and a Resource Book*. Boston: Allyn and Bacon, 2001.

Merrill, Jean. *The Toothpaste Millionaire*. Boston: Houghton Mifflin Company, 1972.

Mitchell, David. *Sticky Note Origami: 25 Designs to Make at Your Desk*. London: PRC Publishing, 2005.

Montroll, John. *Dollar Bill Origami*. Canada: General Publishing Company, LTD., 2003.

Moranville, Sharelle Byars. *A Higher Geometry*. New York: Henry Holt and Company, 2006.

Pappas, Theoni. *Math Stuff*. San Carlos: Wide World Publishing/Tetra, 2002.

Pearsall, Shelley. *All of the Above*. New York: Little, Brown and Company, 2006.

Perl, Teri. *Women and Numbers: Lives of Women Mathematicians plus Discovery Activities*. California: World Wide Publishing/Tetra, 1993.

Reimer, Luetta, and Wilbert Reimer. *Mathematicians Are People, Too: Stories from the Lives of Great Mathematicians*. New Jersey: Pearson, 1990.

Roberts, David, ed. *Pick Me Up: Stuff You Need to Know....* New York: DK Publishing, 2006.

Ross, Catherine Sheldrick. *Squares: Shapes in Math, Science, and Nature*. New York: Kids Can Press, 1996.

Rowling, J. K. *Fantastic Beasts and Where To Find Them*. New York: Arthur A. Levine Books, 2001.

—.*Harry Potter and the Sorcerer's Stone*. New York: Scholastic, 1997.

Schwartz, David M. *If You Hopped Like a Frog*. New York: Scholastic, 1999.

—. *If Dogs Were Dinosaurs*. New York: Scholastic, 2005.

Steen, Lynn Arthur, ed. *Mathematics and Democracy: The Case for Quantitative Literacy*. The Woodrow Wilson National Fellowship Foundation, 2001.

Tumanov, Vladimir. *Jayden's Rescue*. Toronto, Canada: Scholastic Canada Ltd., 2002.

Wallace, Faith H., and K.K. Clark. "Reading Stances in Mathematics: Positioning Students and Texts." *Action in Teacher Education* 27.2 (2005): 68-79.

Westerfield, Scott. *Midnighters: Blue Noon*. New York: Eos Books–HarperCollins Publishers, 2005.

—. *Midnighters: The Secret Hour*. New York: Eos Books–HarperCollins Publishers, 2004.

—. *Midnighters: Touching Darkness*. New York: Eos Books–HarperCollins Publishers, 2004.

Whitin, David J., and Sandra Wilde. *Read Any Good Math Lately?: Children's Books for Mathematical Learning, K-6*. Portsmouth: Heinemann, 1992.

Wyatt, Valerie and Pat Cupples. *The Math Book for Girls and Other Beings Who Count*. Niagara Falls, NY: Kids Can Press, 2000.

Appendix: Recommended Picture Books for Middle Grades Classrooms

Base, Graeme. (2006). *Uno's Garden.* **New York: Abrams Books for Young Readers.**

In dramatically illustrated detail, Uno's garden is transformed from a colorful paradise to a bleak, gray industrial city. The reader quickly sees the results of an imbalance between man and nature. In the process, a numbers game among the animals, plants, and buildings are shown at the top of each page via icons representing the various types. While the text and math is simple, the use of the numbers game is a good application of number sequences and more sophisticated math discussions. The plants decrease by a value of one each page, decreasing arithmetically. The buildings are doubling each page, increasing geometrically. Questions can be raised to determine the pattern for each group, and its respective rate of growth/decay. Students can determine the next number in the sequence, plot the data in a graph, and possibly even write explicit and recursive formulas, etc. *NCTM Standards: Problem Solving, Algebra.*

Ernst, Lisa Campbell, and Lee Ernst. (2005). *Tangram Magician.* **Maplewood, New Jersey: Blue Apple Books.**

In this puzzle activity book based on the Chinese legend, the magician in the story transforms into 25 different forms. Readers can create the forms using the foam Tangram shapes (5 triangles, square, and parallelogram) included with the book, or make a new form of their own design. *NCTM Standards: Geometry and Problem Solving.*

Goldstone, Bruce. (2006). *Great Estimations.* **New York: Henry Holt and Company.**

For years, the art of estimation has only been tested at birthday parties and county fairs (e.g., "Guess how many jellybeans are in the jar."). In this book, numerous objects in various groupings are displayed and techniques for training the eye to "count" them are explained. Making reasonable estimates requires the use of logic, mental math, and quantitative groupings—all skills most young adults would benefit from further training in. *NCTM Standards: Measurement.*

Leedy, Loreen. (2007). *It's Probably Penny.* **New York: Henry Holt and Company.**

An introductory lesson in probability using jellybeans, *It's Probably Penny* demonstrates how to make predictions based on the notion of chance—unequal, equal, tiny, impossible, possible but very unlikely, and "will for sure." This is a good starting point for students to create their own experiments, visualize samples, and determine possible outcomes. *NCTM Standards: Data Analysis and Probability.*

Leedy, Loreen. (2000). *Mapping Penny's World.* **New York: Henry Holt and Company.**

Using information provided on the blackboard by her teacher, Lisa creates maps of her bedroom, home, neighborhood, town, and planet. Although the story may be geared for younger ages, the concepts of scale, proportion, and scale drawings could be introduced using the rudimentary maps as a basis of understanding. *NCTM Standards: Measurement, Numbers and Operations.*

Leedy, Loreen. (1997). *Measuring Penny*. New York: Henry Holt and Company.

In a clearly defined homework assignment provided on the blackboard, Lisa is tasked with measuring something "in as many ways as you can." She decides to measure her dog Penny using ruler, dog biscuits, yardstick, seesaw, scale, thermometer, and stopwatch. This book provides a basic depiction of the use of measurement in height, weight, time, length, width and volume using customary, metric and nonstandard units. *NCTM Standards: Measurement.*

Nagda, Ann Whitehead. (2000). *Panda Math: Learning about Subtraction from Hua Mei and Mei Sheng*. New York: Henry Holt and Company.

Subtraction is explained via the story of mother panda and her newborn cub. Story details including weight, diet, sleep, and life expectancy are incorporated into real-world subtraction word problems. Problems are explained visually using various methods for solving including: base 10, regrouping, place value, and adding up. *NCTM Standards: Numbers and Operations.*

Nagda, Ann Whitehead, and Cindy Bickel. (2004). *Polar Bear Math: Learning about Fractions from Klondike and Snow*. New York: Henry Holt and Company.

Zookeepers at the Denver Zoo must learn how to care for two abandoned polar bear cubs. As we follow their progress, data gleaned from the within the story is provided in fraction format on one side of the book. *Polar Bear Math* uses illustrations and tables to uniquely explain fraction terms such as numerator, denominator, common denominator, equivalent fractions, and the overall concept of a fraction being "part of a whole." Additionally, fraction format is used within the perspective of weight, time, liquid measure, etc. thus enhancing the rich real-world math experience. *NCTM Standards: Numbers and Operations.*

Nagda, Ann Whitehead, and Cindy Bickel. (2000). *Tiger Math: Learning to Graph from a Baby Tiger*. New York: Henry Holt and Company.

Chronicling the growth of a tiger cub in the Denver Zoo, *Tiger Math* provides data and graphs in a relevant context. Picture graphs, pie charts, bar graphs, and line graphs "make it easy to see and understand information about numbers." *NCTM Standards: Data Analysis and Probability.*

Neuschwander, Cindy. (2005). *Mummy Math: An Adventure in Geometry*. New York: Henry Holt and Company.

On a quest to find the mummy of an ancient pharaoh, the characters in the story suddenly become trapped inside a pyramid. Using the colorful hieroglyphics (shaped like geometric solids) and the pharaoh's clues to discover the way out, the story provides a cursory introduction to eight geometric solids. Post-reading activities are included to assist students in classifying and identifying three-dimensional geometric shapes. *NCTM Standards: Geometry and Problem Solving.*

Schwartz, David, and James A. Warhol. (1999). *If You Hopped Like a Frog*. New York: Scholastic Books.

Using fun and relevant comparisons, *If You Hopped Like a Frog* vividly illustrates the concept of ratios and proportions. On each page, a different scenario and outcome is presented. Readers begin to understand, backed by scientific data, how far a human jump if "they jumped like a flea," for example. The back of the book provides examples ideal for individual or group work. *NCTM Standards: Numbers and Operations.*

Silverstein, Shel. (1981). *The Missing Piece Meets the Big O.* **New York: Harper Collins.**

A simple visualization of transformational geometry concepts: translations, rotations and dilations. At one point in the story, the "missing piece" meets a shape he fits into perfectly, but he suddenly begins to grow (dilate.) When the missing piece begins to roll, a connection to rotations and translations can be made. *NCTM Standards: Geometry.*

Smith, David. (2002). *If the World Were a Village: A Book about the World's People.* **Tonawanda, New York: Kids Can Press.**

Scaling the world's 6.2 billion people into a village of 100 provides a more understandable perspective for discussing global issues like clean air and water, literacy, and possessions. It also provides an illuminating background for a discussion on ratios and proportions. "If 22 people in the village of 100 speak a Chinese dialect, how many of Earth's 6.2 billion people speak a Chinese dialect?" Students will come to see the value of using reduced numbers to convey information, and an appreciation for their place in the real global village. *NCTM Standards: Numbers and Operations.*

Tang, G. (2003). *Math Appeal: Mind-Stretching Math Riddles.* **New York: Scholastic.**
Tang, G. (2005). *Math Potatoes: Mind-Stretching Brain Food.* **New York: Scholastic.**

Both *Math Appeal* and *Math Potatoes* challenge the reader's computation and problem-solving skills by providing a group of objects and a riddle hinting to a faster and easier way to determine the sum. In each example, mental math skills are strengthened by grouping in a variety of ways, using multiplication instead of addition, and rounding. Answers and explanations are provided in the back of the book. *NCTM Standards: Numbers and Operations.*

Index

W

www.ingramcontent.com/pod-product-compliance
Lightning Source LLC
Chambersburg PA
CBHW050415110426
42812CB00006BA/1894